The VEGGIE CHINESE Takeaway COOKBOOK

Publishing Director Sarah Lavelle
Assistant Editor Stacey Cleworth
Design & Art Direction Emily Lapworth
Photographer Sam Folan
Food Stylist Emily Jonzen
Props Stylist Agathe Gits
Head of Production Stephen Lang
Production Controller Katie Jarvis

Published in 2020 by Quadrille,
an imprint of Hardie Grant Publishing

Quadrille
52–54 Southwark Street
London SE1 1UN
quadrille.com

Cataloguing in Publication Data: a catalogue record
for this book is available from the British Library.

Text © Kwoklyn Wan 2020
Photography © Sam Folan 2020
Design © Quadrille 2020

ISBN 978-1-78713-509-3

Printed in China

Wok, No Meat?
Over 70 vegan and vegetarian
takeaway classics

The VEGGIE CHINESE Takeaway COOKBOOK

KWOKLYN WAN

Photography by Sam Folan

Hardie Grant

QUADRILLE

6.	Introduction ....
9.	Storecupboard essentials ....
12.	Equipment ....
15.	Menu ideas ....
17.	Chinese Festivals ....

SOUPS

20.	Spice & Sour Soup ....
21.	Veggie Wonton Soup ....
23.	Seaweed & Tofu Soup ....
24.	Tom Yum Soup ....
26.	Creamed Corn Soup ....
27.	Napa Cabbage & Tofu Soup ....

STARTERS & DUMPLINGS

30.	Spring Onion Pancakes ....
33.	Potstickers ....
34.	Phoenix Rolls with Sweet & Sour Dipping Sauce ....
36.	Roll Your Own Summer Rolls ....
39.	Ho Chi Min Fried Spring Rolls ....
40.	Tofu & Vegetable Samsa ....
41.	Mini Spring Rolls ....
42.	Sweet Lotus Bao ....
44.	Tempura Veg with Dipping Sauce ....
46.	Panko Mushrooms with OK Dipping Sauce ....
47.	Sesame Seed Tempura Fried Tofu ....
49.	Griddled Sweet Potato Pancakes ....
50.	Taro, Sesame & Lotus Puk Puks ....
52.	Lotus Root Crisps ....
55.	Cauliflower Yuk Sung ....
56.	Cauliflower Fritters ....
59.	Chinese Beer-battered Pakoda ....

MAINS

62.	Spicy Hoisin Mixed Vegetables ....
65.	Crispy Tofu with Spring Onions ....
66.	Kung Po Cauliflower ....
69.	Chinese Orange Tofu with Peppers & Pineapple ....
70.	Sichuan Pepper Mushrooms ....
71.	Chinese Mushroom Curry ....
72.	Chilli Salt Tofu ....
75.	Cauliflower Steak with a Rich Chinese Gravy ....
76.	Katsu Cauliflower with Tonkatsu Sauce ..
79.	Teriyaki Bowl ....
80.	Hoisin Glazed Tempeh ....
83.	Mapo Tofu ....
84.	Purple Sprouting Broccoli & Peanut Satay Sauce ....
87.	Stir-fried Aubergine with Sesame Seeds ....
88.	Bok Choy with Mushroom Stir-Fry Sauce ....
90.	Mock Char Siu Bao with Pickled Chinese Vegetables ....
92.	Fried Tofu with Chilli & Black Beans ....
93.	Sichuan Crisp Cauliflower ....
94.	Black Pepper Tempeh with Green Peppers & Onions ....
95.	Crispy Chilli Cauliflower ....

RICE

98.	Oven Steamed Rice ....
98.	Jasmine Rice ....
99.	Coconut Rice ....
100.	Eight Treasure Fried Rice ....
103.	Sticky Rice Parcels ....
104.	Rice Porridge Congee ....
106.	Seasoned Glutinous Rice ....
107.	Chinese Baked Rice ....

NOODLES

110.	Hong Kong Crispy Noodles with Mixed Vegetables ....
112.	Vegetable Chow Mein ....
113.	Hong Kong-style Noodle Soup with Tofu & Chinese Vegetables ....

115. Mushroom Lo Mein ....

116. Vegetable Udon in Yellow Bean
Sauce with Cashew Nuts ....

117. Udon Noodles with Five Spice Tofu ....

119. Udon Noodle Curry Soup ....

120. Chilli Tofu Ramen ....

122. Singapore Rice Noodles ....

123. Dan Dan Noodles ....

125. Tofu, Pickled Cabbage &
Black Beans on Rice Noodles ....

126. Hot & Sour Chinese Vegetables
with Mung Bean Noodles ....

129. Stir-fried Ho Fun ....

130. Mushroom Teriyaki with Soba Noodles ..

SIDES

134. Asian Slaw ....

136. Chinese Breadsticks ....

137. Eggless Omelette ....

139. Asparagus with Ginger Soy ....

140. Chinese Broccoli in Garlic
& Ginger Sauce ....

141. Beansprouts with Garlic & Onion ....

142. Spiced Bok Choy ....

143. Chilli Stir-fried Lettuce ....

144. Napa Cabbage with Mushroom Sauce ..

145. Honey Rice Wine Broccoli Stems ....

SAUCES, DIPS & PICKLING

148. Soy Pickled Cucumber ....

151. Sweet Pickled Ginger ....

152. Chinese Pickled Vegetables ....

154. Sweet Chilli Sauce ....

154. Hoisin Sauce ....

155. Mushroom Stir-Fry Sauce ....

156. Index ....

160. Acknowledgements ....

66.

110.

44.

90.

INTRODUCTION

As a third-generation Cantonese chef, having quite literally grown up in the frantically beating heart of the Chinese restaurants and takeaways owned and run by my parents and my grandfather before them, writing my previous book *The Chinese Takeaway Cookbook* felt like a deliciously therapeutic trip down memory lane, reliving my time in the kitchens and recalling the original recipes of the most-ordered Chinese takeaway dishes to share with you. The recipes have been so popular with readers that I regularly receive pictures of the delicious meals that they've prepared for friends and family. In the world of food, nothing makes me happier than to see inspired home cooks trying new recipes and feeling the satisfaction of having created something amazing.

The Chinese Takeaway Cookbook included meat, fish and vegetarian dishes, but when I was asked to write a vegetarian/vegan Chinese takeaway cookbook, I was truly excited to explore more of the flavourful vegetable options. Having taken some time out to investigate what is currently available in the marketplace and expecting to find vibrant veggies in luscious marinades, I was a little confused by the vast array of overseasoned and processed products that were simply 'pretending' to be meat. And so I began to write; taking the freshest of produce, the five flavours of Chinese cookery – salty, spicy, sour, sweet and bitter – and using traditional cooking techniques that, instead of masking the flavours, elevated them to new heights in combination with classic Chinese and Pan-Asian ingredients and seasonings inspired by my childhood and travels.

'One must learn to blend the flavours harmoniously to truly master Chinese cookery.'

CHINESE PROVERB

Whenever I'm in Hong Kong I head to the many temples and monasteries, not only for the complete tranquillity and beauty but also for their amazing vegetarian food. I've found nowhere else that feeds the mind, body and soul in such a peaceful way. Vegetarianism is one of the most important contributions that Buddhist monks have made to Chinese cuisine. Over the centuries they have perfected the preparation and method of these dishes and, as most abstain from all byproducts of meat, fish and eggs, many of these recipes can easily be modified to become completely vegan. From around the thirteenth century the Buddhist community has opened vegetarian restaurants in cities across China and has inspired the creation of a distinct cuisine complete with imitation meats.

Traditional cooking methods include the quick stir-fry in a wok over a very high heat. As soon as the ingredients hit the red-hot surface, they're sealed, locking in all the goodness, and after a mere few minutes more, they're cooked. Preparing such beautiful ingredients can be very therapeutic; take your time to ensure each vegetable is cut to the exact same size, and immerse yourself in the simple pleasure of the preparation – the cooking can be quite frantic as the wok roars, spits and smokes over the lick of the flames.

With a little bit of time, care and preparation, you can extract so much flavour from the simplest of ingredients and no more so than from the humble vegetable.

Whether you're a devout vegan or a carnivore who enjoys a 'graze on the green side', vegetables need no longer be a mere side dish, but should be celebrated in all their glory, whether that be a crispy cauliflower steak dressed in Tonkatsu sauce or a sumptuous seaweed and tofu soup; the world is your... cucumber!

Kwoklyn x
www.kwoklynwan.com

STORECUPBOARD ESSENTIALS

Sesame oil

Add the tiniest amount of this oil, extracted from the humble sesame seed, to marinades or at the very end of cooking to quite literally transform your dish from yum to OMG nom, nom, nom. Use sparingly as it's packed with flavour and can overpower if used too liberally. Where possible buy pure sesame oil and not the blended variety.

Light soy sauce

The light variety is used to season your dish or as a dip; it's saltier than its darker sibling but is still packed with that umami flavour that we all love. It's made using fermented soya bean paste.

Dark soy sauce

Sweeter and thicker than its lighter sibling and packed with umami to bring a silky smoothness to our taste buds as well as to colour dishes and inject flavour. Made using fermented soya beans, molasses and sweetener agents, it is aged for longer than the lighter variety.

Mushroom stir-fry sauce

Used widely to inject some serious flavour into a dish. Made with dried Chinese mushrooms, seaweed and soy sauce, it's packed with that unctuous umami taste that is very often found in Chinese cuisine (page 155).

Chinese five spice

Made by combining star anise, Sichuan peppercorns, cinnamon, fennel seeds and cloves, the ingredients are ground to a fine powder to create this well-loved and frequently used seasoning. Used to flavour many dishes but especially those that originate from Cantonese cuisine.

Sichuan pepper

Sichuan pepper's unique flavour is not spicy or pungent but lemony; its unique characteristic is the tingly numbing sensation that it produces in the mouth as you eat. It is very often used in combination with fresh chillies and star anise in Sichuan cuisine.

Rice vinegar

Clear rice vinegar is made by fermenting rice, firstly into alcohol and then into acid; compared to white distilled vinegar it is less acidic and sweeter in flavour. Black vinegar is made with glutinous rice and aged longer to produce a woody, smoky malt flavour and is widely used in southern Chinese cuisine.

Rice wine

Made from the fermentation of rice starch that has been converted into sugars and is used widely in Asian cooking. Typically, it has an alcohol content of 18–25 per cent.

THE HOLY TRINITY

There are three key ingredients you need when cooking Cantonese food: garlic, ginger and spring onions. They are sometimes used all together and sometimes they appear on their own but you'll always find at least one when cooking traditional Cantonese cuisine.

Garlic cloves

Garlic cloves pack a serious amount of flavour and are closely related to onions, chives and leeks. Originating in central Asia, garlic is widely used across the world as a seasoning for its pungent flavour.

Ginger root

Ginger root has been used in China for millennia as a medicine; closely related to turmeric and cardamom it originates from the islands of South East Asia. Its flavour is hot and fragrant and can be prepared for consumption in many ways, including pickling, steeping in tea, candied or used as an ingredient for cooking.

Spring onions

Spring onions have a milder taste than their related cousins, onions, chives, shallots and garlic. The entire plant is edible, raw or cooked, and the hollow leaves are used as a vegetable in many dishes around the world.

Tip for using these three Cantonese flavours: if you want a subtle hint of flavour, chop the ingredients into large pieces; as they cook they will slowly infuse the dish with their aromatic yumminess. For a full-bodied kapow hit of flavour, finely chop the ingredients so that every mouthful holds an aromatic explosion.

EQUIPMENT

Wok

The round-bottomed wok was designed to sit over a hollow, above a roaring-hot fire. Made from thinly beaten carbon steel, the entire surface of the wok reaches a high temperature, making it perfect for the style of cooking known as stir-frying. Over time the wok builds up layers of oil; this is known as 'seasoning'. The seasoning of a wok makes the carbon-steel surface non-stick and food literally glides across the surface as it cooks. You may find that when you buy a new wok, food will stick to it, but over time and with the layer of 'seasoning' the wok will create a charred flavour and aroma. If you are using a seasoned wok you must never use it for boiling or steaming as it will break down the seasoning and your wok will begin to stick again.

Chopsticks

Have you ever noticed that when you eat Chinese food everything is already cut into bite-sized pieces? For the Chinese, having to cut up your food at the table is seen as uncivilised; this notion dates back to the Zhou dynasty, which was over 2,000 years ago. Chopsticks are used as eating utensils in virtually all Asian countries. Held in the dominant hand, they are of equal length, smooth and usually tapered at the end. The invention of chopsticks reflects the wisdom of ancient Chinese people. A pair of chopsticks, though they look simple, can nip, pick, rip and stir food. Nowadays, chopsticks are considered to be lucky gifts for marriage and other important ceremonies.

Strainer/sieve

Also known as the Chinese spider strainer, this is an invaluable piece of equipment when frying or boiling noodles or dumplings in a wok. The handle is often made of bamboo while the strainer itself is made of metal and sometimes brass. It's been vital in all the Chinese restaurants and takeaways I've worked in; the Chinese kitchen just wouldn't work without one.

Knife or chopper

Over the years I have become an avid collector of Chinese kitchen knives, also known as a chopper. When choosing your chopper, you want to look for a thin, lightweight blade that will chop through vegetables evenly; if your chopper is too thick, you'll struggle to do the intricate slicing that many recipes require. Once you've invested in a good knife, it's important to look after it; sharpen it each time you use it and make sure it is completely dry after washing. A sharp knife really does make all the difference – nothing is quite as satisfying than feeling the blade glide effortlessly through your ingredients as you prepare them for your meal.

Bamboo steamer

The bamboo steamer steams the food in tiers and is designed to sit snugly inside your wok. Developed over thousands of years in China the bamboo steamer is a practical kitchen accessory you will use time and time again.

MENU IDEAS

PARTY CANAPÉS

Believe it or not, it's so simple to create amazing bite-sized treats (many of which, I hasten to add, your guests will have never tried before) using recipes from this book. I've organised them into two groups: bowl canapés that can be two or three mouthfuls served in a tiny bowl or Chinese teacup, and bite-sized canapés that you eat with your fingers.

Bowl canapés

Hot & Sour Chinese Vegetables with Mung Bean Noodles (page 126) – simply chop your vegetables into smaller pieces; you could even add small pieces of fried tofu to the vegetables.

Teriyaki Bowl (page 79) – follow the recipe but chop the vegetables into smaller pieces and serve on top of bite-sized mounds of Oven Steamed Rice (page 98).

Chilli Tofu Ramen (page 120) – cut the tofu into smaller pieces and serve with just a small swirl of noodles in the bottom of the bowl.

Bite-sized canapés

Ho Chi Min Fried Spring Rolls (page 39) – follow the recipe, cut each cooked spring roll into three and wrap in a lettuce leaf once cooled.

Cauliflower Fritters (page 56) – simply make the fritters smaller and serve with Hoisin Sauce (page 154).

Taro, Sesame and Lotus Puk Puks (page 50) – these are the perfect size just as they are.

A ROMANTIC DINNER FOR TWO

The art of a stress-free romantic dinner for two is all in the preparation; you'll be amazed at just how much of the meal you can prepare way in advance of the meal itself.

Soup

Spice & Sour Soup (page 20) – make this in advance, leaving out the cornflour, egg and sesame oil. Once the soup begins to boil, turn off the heat, pop on a lid and allow to cool. Just before serving bring back to a simmer and then add the cornflour mixture to thicken. Remove from the heat, then add the egg and the sesame oil.

Starter

Roll Your Own Summer Rolls (page 36) – follow the recipe, arrange the rolls on your serving plates and cover with cling film (plastic wrap). When you are ready to serve you'll need a small bowl of warm water to soften the rolls.

Main course

Vegetable Udon in Yellow Bean Sauce with Cashew Nuts (page 116) – prepare all of your ingredients ahead of time. This dish literally takes 5 minutes to cook once everything is ready.

Dessert

Fresh oranges – the Chinese often finish with a plate of fresh oranges as a palate cleanser.

EASY ENTERTAINING SUPPER CLUB

Supper clubs are growing in popularity; having organised and been a guest chef at quite a few, I'd like to think I'm now a dab hand at these events.

Canapés

Please see the previous page for ideas – all can be made in advance and served at room temperature.

Starters

Panko Mushrooms with OK Dipping Sauce (page 46) – follow the steps in the recipe to pre-fry your mushrooms then place on a wire rack to cool. Just before service you can either warm the mushrooms in a low oven or flash-fry them. The sauce is served at room temperature.

Main course

Udon Noodle Curry Soup (page 119) – make the soup in advance and allow to cool. Prepare the garnish. When you are ready to serve, reheat the soup while you cook the noodles. Put the noodles into serving bowls, pour over the soup and finish with the spring onion garnish.

CHINESE FESTIVALS

Chinese New Year

Chinese New Year, also known as the spring festival, is celebrated on the first of fifteen full moons in the Chinese lunar calendar; unlike the Gregorian calendar the date changes each year. It's the largest celebration in China; during the celebrations, food plays a massive part with banquets being served including some dishes that are considered to be very lucky. Potstickers (page 33) and Mini Spring Rolls (page 41) are served for wealth, and noodles (pages 108–131) are served for happiness and longevity.

The Lantern Festival

The Lantern Festival is celebrated on the 15th day of the first lunar month; traditionally rice balls with various fillings are eaten on this day, while homes, offices and streets are decorated with Chinese lanterns.

The Dragon Boat Festival

The Dragon Boat Festival is an important celebration in China to commemorate Qu Yuan, a famous patriotic poet of China in ancient times. The symbolism of Sticky Rice Parcels (page 103) is based on the legend of Qu Yuan, who drowned himself in the Miluo River on hearing that his state was defeated. It's said that people threw rice parcels into the river to feed the fish, so they would leave Qu Yuan's body in peace.

Mid Autumn Festival

Mid Autumn Festival, also known as the Moon Festival, is celebrated on the 15th day of the eighth lunar month and is China's second-largest celebration. It takes its name from always being celebrated in the autumn season at the time when the moon is at its fullest and brightest. Mooncakes are presented to family members to wish them long and happy lives. The thin, tender pastry envelops a sweet, dense filling of red bean or lotus seed paste and may hold at the centre yolks from salted duck eggs to symbolise the full moon. Mooncakes are usually eaten in small wedges accompanied by tea.

SOUPS

SPICE & SOUR SOUP

This soup is rich, tangy and spicy; a complete mouth sensation that will satisfy any craving. Along with the crunchy carrots and soft tofu it really packs a punch in the flavour and texture departments.

15 MINUTES　　**10 MINUTES**　　**SERVES 2–4**

5g (¼ cup) dried wood ear mushrooms, cut into matchsticks
½ Tbsp dark soy sauce
1 Tbsp light soy sauce
8 Tbsp rice vinegar
2 dried chillies, finely chopped
30g (1oz) firm tofu, cubed
1 medium carrot, cut into matchsticks
30g (¼ cup) canned bamboo shoots, drained and cut into matchsticks
30g (¼ cup) peas
4 eggs, beaten (omit for vegan option)
1.8 litres (7 cups) vegetable stock
½ tsp white pepper
1½ tsp salt
1 Tbsp sugar
4 Tbsp tomato ketchup
1 Tbsp tomato purée (paste)
3 Tbsp cornflour (cornstarch) mixed with 6 Tbsp water
½ Tbsp sesame oil

Soak the mushrooms in warm water for 10 minutes, then drain and transfer to a large wok or saucepan. Add the dark and light soy sauces, rice vinegar, dried chillies, tofu, carrot, bamboo shoots, peas, half the beaten eggs, vegetable stock, seasonings, sugar, ketchup and purée into the pan with the mushrooms. Slowly bring to the boil, then reduce the heat and simmer for 3 minutes.

Give the cornflour and water a good mix, then turn the heat up to medium and slowly add the mixture to the soup, stirring constantly until you reach the desired consistency. Remove from the heat and slowly pour in the remaining beaten eggs, stirring as you pour. Finally add the sesame oil and serve.

VEGGIE WONTON SOUP

The Chinese describe wontons as 'little clouds', floating gently in a rich aromatic broth of ginger and spring onion (two of the Holy Trinity of Cantonese flavours).

30 MINUTES   **10 MINUTES**   **SERVES 2–4**

For the wontons

1 bag (approx. 260g/9¼oz) fresh spinach

10g (½ cup) dried wood ear mushrooms, soaked in warm water for 10 minutes

60g (2oz) medium firm tofu

3 spring onions (scallions), finely chopped

1 Tbsp sesame oil

1 Tbsp grated fresh ginger

¼ tsp white pepper

1 tsp cornflour (cornstarch)

pinch of salt

16–20 wonton wrappers

For the soup

3cm (1¼in) piece of fresh ginger, cut into thin slices

1 Tbsp soy sauce

800ml (3⅓ cups) vegetable stock

½ tsp white pepper

1 tsp salt

1 spring onion (scallion), finely chopped

1 tsp sesame oil

For the wontons, heat a wok over a medium heat and add the fresh spinach, until wilted. Then transfer the wilted spinach to kitchen paper, squeeze out the excess water and then roughly chop and place into a large bowl. Finely chop the mushrooms and tofu into small pieces and add to the bowl, together with the remainder of the wonton ingredients, except the wrappers, and mix well.

To assemble the wontons, place a wonton wrapper in the palm of your hand and spoon a ½ tablespoon of mixture into the centre. Carefully fold the sides of the wrapper keeping the filling in the centre and pinch the wrapper just above the ball of mixture to seal. Continue with the remaining wrappers and filling until you have made all the wontons. Set aside while you make the soup.

In a deep saucepan, add the ginger, soy sauce, stock, white pepper and salt and bring to the boil. Then turn down the heat and leave to simmer for 8–10 minutes.

While the soup simmers, bring a large saucepan of water to the boil, then carefully drop the wontons into the boiling water and cook for 2–3 minutes.

Divide the cooked wontons between bowls, sprinkle with the chopped spring onion and add a drizzle of sesame oil. Pour over the hot soup and serve.

SEAWEED & TOFU SOUP

This nourishing seaweed soup is packed with flavour, as well as being full of vitamins and minerals. Seaweed is a great source of umami and along with the crunch of bamboo shoots, the crisp snap of carrot batons and the subtle background heat from the pepper, this dish delivers on taste time and time again.

10 MINUTES   **10 MINUTES**   **SERVES 2–4**

1 litre (4 cups) vegetable stock
300g (10oz) firm tofu, cubed
1 medium carrot, cut into matchsticks
60g (½ cup) canned bamboo shoots, drained and cut into matchsticks
3cm (1¼in) piece of fresh ginger, cut into 3 slices
¼ tsp white pepper
2 Tbsp light soy sauce
1 Tbsp dark soy sauce
1 Tbsp cornflour (cornstarch) mixed with 2 Tbsp water
1 egg white, beaten (omit for vegan option)
4 nori seaweed sheets, cut into 2cm (¾in) squares
½ Tbsp sesame oil

Put the vegetable stock into a large saucepan along with the tofu, carrot, bamboo shoots, ginger, white pepper and light and dark soy sauces. Bring to a gentle simmer and allow to cook for 5 minutes.

Gradually add the cornflour mixture, stirring constantly until the mixture is smooth enough to coat the back of a spoon. Remove from the heat and quickly stir in the beaten egg white, if using. Finally, add the nori squares and a splash of sesame oil and stir through the soup. Check the seasoning before serving.

TOM YUM SOUP

Although this dish originates from Thai cuisine, it has been widely served in many Chinese takeaways across the world. This is a deliciously nourishing soup that is spicy, sour and creamy, with a rich tang from the tomatoes and lime juice.

10 MINUTES **30 MINUTES** **SERVES 2–4**

2 lemongrass stalks
2 red bird's-eye chillies, finely chopped
3 garlic cloves, roughly chopped
1 Tbsp grated fresh ginger
1 Tbsp oil (vegetable, groundnut or coconut)
1.5 litres (6 cups) vegetable stock
2–3 medium tomatoes, diced
1 x 400ml (14fl oz) can coconut milk
5 lime leaves (or use 1½ Tbsp grated lime zest)
3 Tbsp light soy sauce
220g (8oz) firm tofu, cubed
60g (1 cup) button mushrooms, sliced
¼ cup lime juice
1½ Tbsp demerara sugar
½ tsp salt (or to taste)

Trim the top leaves of the lemongrass and using the flat of your knife or a pestle, bruise the entire length of each stalk to get the most of the citrusy flavour, then cut the stalks into quarters. Use a pestle and mortar to grind the chillies, garlic and ginger to a paste.

Heat the oil in a large saucepan over a medium heat and fry the lemongrass and chilli, garlic and ginger paste for about 3 minutes until fragrant. Add the vegetable stock, tomatoes, coconut milk, lime leaves and soy sauce and mix well, then bring to the boil. Reduce the heat to a simmer, cover and cook for 15 minutes.

Add the tofu and mushrooms to the pan and cook for a further 8 minutes before adding the lime juice and sugar, and seasoning with salt to taste. Serve and enjoy.

CREAMED CORN SOUP

This soup hits all the right notes: warm, comforting, savoury –
and yet it still has a deliciously subtle sweetness. Traditionally
Cantonese, this soup can be found in many Chinese restaurants, it's
also particularly popular in Chinese takeaways across the world.

5 MINUTES   **10 MINUTES**   **SERVES 2–4**

800ml (3⅓ cups) vegetable stock
1 x 400g (14oz) can creamed corn
¼ tsp white pepper
30g (¼ cup) peas
2 Tbsp cornflour (cornstarch) mixed
    with 4 Tbsp water
1 egg, beaten (omit for vegan option)
1 tsp sesame oil
salt, to taste

Put the vegetable stock into a medium saucepan and bring to the
boil. Add the creamed corn and bring back to the boil, then reduce
to a gentle simmer and season with the white pepper and salt to
taste. Add the peas and return to the boil.

Stir the cornflour and water until it is smooth enough to coat the back
of a spoon. While the soup is boiling, gradually add the cornflour
mixture, stirring constantly. Turn the heat down and slowly pour in
the beaten egg (if using), stirring the soup at the same time. Pour the
soup into serving bowls, add a drizzle of sesame oil and serve.

NAPA CABBAGE & TOFU SOUP

This is the Chinese version of a hearty vegetable soup. Presentation is key as this soup is served in its cooking pot – you want to see each ingredient in its own section of the pot; this not only looks amazing but as you eat you are able to identify the individual ingredients before they combine to create that perfect mouthful.

10 MINUTES   **20 MINUTES**   **SERVES 2–4**

1 litre (4 cups) vegetable stock
1cm (½in) piece of fresh ginger, cut into thin slices
½ tsp salt (or to taste)
¼ tsp white pepper (or to taste)
150g (5oz) daikon radish (mooli), cut into bite-sized pieces
3 spring onions (scallions), halved and thinly sliced lengthways
200g (7oz) Napa cabbage (Chinese leaf), cut into bite-sized pieces
handful of golden needle mushrooms (enoki), hard stalks removed and separated
200g (7oz) firm tofu, cubed
1 nori seaweed sheet, ground to a powder

Pour the vegetable stock into a medium saucepan, add the sliced ginger and bring to the boil. Add the salt and white pepper and stir through the soup, then add the daikon radish and spring onions and allow to simmer for 5 minutes. Next, add the Napa cabbage, mushrooms and tofu into the soup, each in its own part of the pan. Cook for another 8 minutes with the lid on. Turn off the heat, remove the lid and season to taste. Serve at the table in the pan, finally sprinkling with the powdered nori as you ladle into serving bowls.

STARTERS
&
DUMPLINGS

SPRING ONION PANCAKES

Cong you bing, or spring onion pancakes, are a very popular addition to many dim sum menus across China. Not dissimilar to the Indian paratha, this pan-fried unleavened bread is crispy on the outside, chewy on the inside and totally moreish.

1 HOUR   **20 MINUTES**   **SERVES 4**

For the pancakes
250g (2 cups) plain (all-purpose) flour, plus extra for dusting
500–750ml (2–3 cups) boiling water (this will vary slightly depending on the flour you use so adjust accordingly)

For the filling
4 Tbsp coconut oil or vegetable lard, plus extra for brushing
6 spring onions (scallions), thinly sliced
½ tsp Chinese five spice
pinch of salt
pinch of white pepper
2 Tbsp plain (all-purpose) flour
1 Tbsp sesame seeds

For the dough, put the flour into a large bowl and carefully pour over 500ml (2 cups) boiling water, then mix with a fork, until no more water can be seen. You may need to add a little more water if the mixture is still too dry – you want the flour to come together to form a dough ball. Once cool enough to handle, knead the dough on a clean flat surface, until it is smooth and not at all sticky. Set to one side and allow to rest for 45 minutes while you get started on the filling.

Heat 2 tablespoons of the coconut oil or vegetable lard in a wok, add the spring onions and five spice and cook for 1 minute. Add a pinch of salt and pepper, then sprinkle over the flour and cook for 2 minutes over a medium-low heat. Set to one side and allow to cool.

Heat a dry wok over a medium-high heat, add the sesame seeds and toast until golden brown. Transfer to a plate to cool.

After your dough has rested for 45 minutes, knead for a further 1 minute and then cut into 4 equal pieces. Take one piece and roll into a rectangle about 3mm (⅛in) thick. Brush with coconut oil, spread a thin layer of filling over the entire rectangle, then lightly sprinkle with sesame seeds. Starting at one end roll the full length of the dough into a long sausage shape, then coil into a pinwheel, tucking the loose end underneath. Using the palm of your hand lightly roll to flatten each pinwheel to around 5mm (¼in) thick. Repeat with the remainder of the ingredients.

Heat the remaining coconut oil or vegetable lard in a flat-bottomed wok over a medium heat and fry each pancake for 2–3 minutes on each side, flipping a few times to ensure they do not burn. Drain on kitchen paper while you cook the rest. Cut into quarters and serve on their own or with your favourite dipping sauce.

POTSTICKERS

The Chinese have a serious love affair with these succulent and juicy dumplings. Pan-fried and then steamed, every mouthful is sheer perfection.

1-2 HOURS   **30 MINUTES**   **32 DUMPLINGS**

For the dumpling wrappers
280g (2¼ cups) plain (all-purpose) flour
175ml (¾ cup) just-boiled water

For the filling
5 Tbsp oil (vegetable, groundnut or coconut)
1 Tbsp grated fresh ginger
1 large onion, finely diced
1 large portobello mushroom, finely diced
20g (1 cup) dried Chinese mushrooms, soaked in warm water until soft, de-stalked and diced
150g (5oz) Napa cabbage (Chinese leaf), finely chopped
1 carrot, finely diced
5 spring onions (scallions), thinly sliced into rounds
2 Tbsp light soy sauce
2 Tbsp Chinese rice wine
2 tsp sugar
½ tsp white pepper
¾ tsp salt (or to taste)
2 tsp sesame oil

Put the flour into a large bowl and using a wooden spoon add the water in a steady stream, stirring as you go. Start to work the dough into a ball with your hands. Tip the ball out on to a clean un-floured surface and knead until the dough is smooth and not at all sticky.

Place the dough into a ziplock bag and squeeze the air out before sealing. Leave for at least 15 minutes (or up to 2 hours) at room temperature, while you prepare the filling. Add 2 tablespoons of the oil to a wok and place over a medium heat. Fry the ginger until fragrant, then add the onion and cook until the onion is translucent. Add the portobello and Chinese mushrooms and fry until the liquid in the wok has evaporated. Transfer to a bowl.

Wipe the wok and add another tablespoon of oil. Add the cabbage and carrot and fry over a medium heat until any liquid has evaporated. Add the cooked mushrooms, along with the spring onions, soy sauce, Chinese rice wine, sugar, white pepper and salt and mix well. Remove from the heat, stir through the sesame oil and transfer to a large bowl to cool.

Divide the dough into 32 equal pieces using a sharp knife. Roll each piece into a ball before flattening with the heel of your hand. Take a lightly floured rolling pin (to prevent sticking) and roll the dough into thin discs.

To assemble the potstickers, take a teaspoon of filling and place it in the centre of a wrapper, then fold one edge over to meet the other. Gently press the edges together, making sure that no filling escapes, and pinch the sealed edge to form ripples. Place on a sheet of greaseproof paper until you are ready to cook.

Heat the remaining 2 tablespoons of oil in a flat-bottomed wok over a medium-high heat. Add a batch of potstickers and allow to fry on one side only for 2 minutes, then add 5mm (¼in) water, reduce the heat to medium-low and cover with the lid. Allow to steam until the water has evaporated. Remove the lid, increase the heat to medium-high and fry until the potsticker bottoms are golden brown and crispy. Repeat with the next batch until they are all cooked. Serve with your favourite dipping sauce.

PHOENIX ROLLS WITH SWEET & SOUR DIPPING SAUCE

I'm not exactly sure who invented this recipe but I like to think it was my dad. Phoenix rolls always featured on our menu and were a very popular dish. Crispy fried bread wrapped around creamy tofu, juicy mushrooms and soft egg, served with a rich tangy sweet and sour sauce – you have just got to try this recipe.

25 MINUTES   **10 MINUTES**   **SERVES 3–5**

5 slices of fresh white bread, crusts removed
240g (8½oz) firm tofu
1 large portobello mushroom, de-stalked
250ml (1 cup) oil for shallow frying (vegetable, groundnut or coconut)
3 eggs, beaten (for a vegan alternative see the eggless omelette on page 137)
beaten egg (or eggless omelette mixture), for sealing

For the sweet and sour sauce
125ml (½ cup) orange juice
125ml (½ cup) water
3 Tbsp sugar
1 Tbsp tomato purée (paste)
1 Tbsp tomato ketchup
3 Tbsp rice vinegar
2 Tbsp cornflour (cornstarch) mixed with 4 Tbsp water

First make the sauce. Place a large saucepan over a medium heat and add the orange juice, water, sugar, tomato purée, ketchup and rice vinegar. Bring to the boil and then simmer for 5 minutes.

Add the cornflour mixture to the sauce, stirring continuously, until it is smooth enough to coat the back of a spoon. Remove from the heat.

To make the phoenix rolls, use a rolling pin to flatten the bread slices. Cut the tofu into 1cm (½in) thick strips, to the same length as the rolled-out bread and set both to one side. Shallow fry the mushroom in a little oil over a medium heat until tender and golden brown. Once cooled cut into strips around 1cm (½in) thick.

Heat 1 tablespoon of the oil in a non-stick frying pan over a medium-high heat. Add the 3 beaten eggs and cook for around 2 minutes, or until the eggs have set and the bottom is beginning to colour. Carefully flip the omelette over and cook for a further 1–2 minutes. Once cooled, cut the omelette into strips around 1cm (½in) thick (or see the eggless omelette below).

To assemble the rolls, lay the bread on a flat surface, then add a strip of tofu, followed by slices of mushroom and omelette. Starting from the edge closest to you, roll the bread over the ingredients to form a sausage shape. Dip your finger into the single beaten egg (or eggless omelette mixture) and wet the last 2cm (¾in) of the bread to seal. Repeat with the remaining ingredients.

Pour enough oil into a deep-sided frying pan to shallow fry the phoenix rolls and place over a medium-high heat. When the temperature of the oil is about 170°C (340°F) carefully place the phoenix rolls in the pan and cook for 2–3 minutes, or until golden brown all over. You'll need to flip them a couple of times during cooking to ensure even browning. Transfer to kitchen paper and allow to cool for 5 minutes. Cut the phoenix rolls into 5 equal pieces and serve with the dipping sauce.

ROLL YOUR OWN SUMMER ROLLS

Searching for that perfect sharing dish? Look no further. I've served this Pan-Asian dish many times and it's always been a huge success; the conversation flows, fingers get sticky and the sounds of contented murmurs as your guests tuck into their own creations is sublime.

10 MINUTES   **5 MINUTES**   **SERVES 3-5**

For the filling
2 nests of glass (mung bean) noodles
10 rice paper rounds, 22cm (9in) in diameter
½ red (bell) pepper, thinly sliced into strips
1 carrot, thinly sliced into strips
⅓ cucumber, de-seeded and thinly sliced into strips
3 spring onions (scallions), halved and thinly sliced into strips
1 round lettuce, thinly sliced into strips
¼ cup Thai basil leaves (or use regular basil), thinly sliced into strips

For the peanut sauce
2 Tbsp sesame seeds
½ Tbsp oil (vegetable, groundnut or coconut)
3 Tbsp finely diced onion
1 garlic clove, finely chopped
1 tsp dried chilli flakes
2 Tbsp light soy sauce
3 Tbsp smooth peanut butter
1 Tbsp sesame oil
1 Tbsp muscovado sugar (or use maple syrup, agave syrup or brown rice syrup)
3 Tbsp water

Put the glass noodles into a large bowl, pour over boiling water and leave to soak for 3–5 minutes. Once the noodles are soft, drain and set to one side.

Now make the sauce. Place a wok over a medium-low heat; ensure it is completely dry by wiping with kitchen paper before you start. Add the sesame seeds and slowly toast for 2–3 minutes, or until they have turned golden brown. Transfer to a plate and allow to cool. Add the oil to the wok and fry the onion, garlic and chilli flakes over a medium heat until softened, then add the remaining sauce ingredients, including the toasted sesame seeds. Mix well and simmer for 1 minute. Remove from the heat.

To assemble the rolls, soak a rice paper round in warm water for 20–30 seconds, or until soft and pliable. Shake off the excess water and lay flat on a clean work surface or large plate. Arrange your desired fillings in a line in the bottom third of the rice paper round and drizzle with peanut sauce. Fold the bottom third of the rice paper over the filling, then fold the loose side edges over the top before continuing to roll until you have a tightly wrapped parcel of deliciousness.

To enjoy this as a sharing dish, place all of the prepared ingredients in the centre of the table and invite your guests to dip and roll their own, filling with their personal choice of vegetables and sauce.

HO CHI MIN FRIED SPRING ROLLS

Growing up in my parents' restaurant, these Pan-Asian rolls were my all-time favourite dish. Crispy rice paper spring rolls stuffed with crunchy peppers, crisp beansprouts and noodles, all wrapped up in an ice-cold lettuce leaf and then dipped in a sweet, tangy chilli sauce – sheer heaven.

45 MINUTES **45 MINUTES** **SERVES 3–5**

2 nests of glass (mung bean) noodles
1 Tbsp sesame seeds
1 Tbsp oil (vegetable, groundnut or coconut), plus extra for shallow frying
1 Tbsp light soy sauce
1 Tbsp dark soy sauce
2 Tbsp Sriracha chilli sauce
1 tsp Chinese five spice
1 tsp ground Sichuan pepper
½ tsp salt
225g (8oz) firm tofu, cut into 5mm (¼in) slices
10 rice paper rounds, 22cm (9in) in diameter
½ red (bell) pepper, thinly sliced into strips
1 carrot, thinly sliced into strips
3 spring onions (scallions), halved and thinly sliced into strips
small handful of beansprouts
1 round lettuce, leaves separated, washed and drained, to serve

For the sweet chilli vinegar dip
125ml (½ cup) water
125ml (½ cup) rice vinegar
50g (¼ cup) sugar
4 Tbsp honey (or use agave or maple syrup)
1 tsp grated fresh ginger
½ tsp grated garlic
1 red bird's-eye chilli, finely chopped
1 tsp tomato ketchup

Put the glass noodles into a large bowl, cover with boiling water and leave to soak for 3–5 minutes. Once the noodles are soft, drain and set to one side.

To make the sweet chilli vinegar dip, combine all the ingredients in a saucepan, bring to the boil and then simmer for 3–5 minutes until slightly reduced and sticky.

Place a wok over a medium-low heat. Add the sesame seeds and slowly toast for 2–3 minutes, until they have turned golden brown. Transfer to a plate and allow to cool.

Put the oil, soy sauces, Sriracha, Chinese five spice, Sichuan pepper and salt into a large bowl and mix well. Arrange the tofu slices on a shallow plate, then evenly coat the top of the tofu slices with the marinade, keeping some of the marinade for later. Set to one side and leave for 20 minutes.

Preheat the oven to 180°C (350°F). Lay the marinated tofu pieces on a baking tray and bake for 10–15 minutes. Turn the tofu over, cover with the remaining marinade and bake for a further 10–12 minutes. Remove from the oven and allow to cool. Once cooled, cut the tofu into 5mm (¼in) strips.

To assemble the rolls, soak a rice paper round in warm water for 20–30 seconds. Shake off any excess water and lay flat on a clean work surface. Add strips of vegetables and tofu, a sprinkle of sesame seeds and some glass noodles. Fold both sides over the filling, then roll up the rice paper to form a sausage shape.

Heat 250ml (1 cup) oil in a deep-sided frying pan over a medium heat. Carefully fry the rolls, turning them frequently so that they cook evenly, until golden brown all over. Drain on kitchen paper. To eat, take a round lettuce leaf and place one crispy roll in the centre, wrapping the leaf snugly around the roll. Then dip!

TOFU & VEGETABLE SAMSA

So, who knew that East Asia had pyramids? These beautifully formed parcels were designed and created to replicate the Pyramid of Qin Shi Huang, the first emperor of China. A crispy outer shell representing the building itself is stuffed with creamy tofu, crunchy carrots, soft sweet potato and aromatic spices to represent the as-yet undiscovered riches hidden within.

45 MINUTES   **20 MINUTES**   **MAKES 12-14**

400g (14oz) sweet potato, cut into 2cm (¾in) cubes

1 large carrot, cut into 1cm (½in) dice

1 Tbsp oil (vegetable, groundnut or coconut), plus extra for deep-frying

1 Tbsp grated fresh ginger, minced

1 medium onion, finely diced

2 tsp curry powder (use your favourite)

½ tsp ground turmeric

½ tsp ground cumin

½ tsp ground coriander

1 tsp salt

40g (⅓ cup) frozen peas

225g (8oz) firm tofu, drained and crumbled

5 spring onions (scallions), finely chopped

1 Tbsp lemon juice

2 Tbsp water

10–15 spring roll wrappers (25cm/10in square), each cut into 3 equal-sized rectangles

Place the sweet potato and carrot into a large saucepan, cover with water and bring to the boil. Cook for 5 minutes, then remove from the heat, drain and set to one side.

Heat the tablespoon of oil in a wok over a medium-high heat and fry the ginger for 20 seconds until fragrant. Add the onion and fry for about 2 minutes, until translucent. Add the cooked sweet potato and carrots along with the curry powder, turmeric, cumin, coriander and salt and fry for 2 minutes, gently combining the ingredients. Carefully stir in the peas, tofu, spring onions, lemon juice and water. Cook for a further 5 minutes, then transfer to a bowl and allow to cool.

Taking a rectangle of spring roll wrapper, place a heaped teaspoon of the filling in the centre at the top of the wrapper. Brush the outer edges of the wrapper with water and then fold repeatedly from one edge to the other along the length of the strip to form a triangle. Pinch the edges and all the corners to make sure they are sealed tight (you don't want the filling to leak out). Repeat until the filling is used up.

Heat enough oil in a large saucepan to deep-fry the samsa to 180°C (350°F). Fry the samsa in batches for 5 minutes each, turning a couple of times during cooking to achieve an even golden brown colour. Transfer to kitchen paper and serve warm or cold.

MINI SPRING ROLLS

Spring rolls are served during the Spring Festival in China, hence their name. Each perfectly formed roll is packed with seasonal vegetables combined with rich aromatic sauces, creating perfect mouthfuls as you bite through the crispy fried shells.

30 MINUTES   **15 MINUTES**   **SERVES 3–4**

1 nest of glass (mung bean) noodles

1 Tbsp oil (vegetable, groundnut or coconut), plus extra for deep-frying

5 spring onions (scallions), halved and thinly sliced lengthways

1 Tbsp grated fresh ginger

2 garlic cloves, crushed

1 large carrot, cut into thin matchsticks

1 x 220g (8oz) can water chestnuts, drained and roughly chopped

1 x 220g (8oz) can bamboo shoots, drained and cut into thin matchsticks

2 handfuls of beansprouts

1 Tbsp light soy sauce

½ tsp salt

½ tsp white pepper

2 tsp sesame oil

20 spring roll wrappers (21.5cm/8½in square), defrosted

2 Tbsp cornflour (cornstarch) mixed with 1 Tbsp water

Sweet Chilli Sauce (page 154), to serve

Soak the nest of mung bean noodles in a bowl of hot water for 5 minutes, drain and set to one side.

Heat a wok over high heat until hot and add the tablespoon of oil. Add the spring onions, ginger, garlic and carrot and stir-fry for 2–3 minutes until soft. Add the water chestnuts, bamboo shoots, beansprouts, soy sauce, salt and pepper. Stir-fry for a further minute, then turn off heat, stir in the mung bean noodles and drizzle with the sesame oil. Transfer to a bowl and allow to cool.

Place a spring roll wrapper on a board with a corner pointing towards you and brush the edges with the cornflour and water mixture. Put a tablespoon of vegetable mixture on to the wrapper just below the middle and towards the corner closest to you. Fold the tip of the corner up and over the filling creating an 8cm (3in) sausage shape, then fold in the two side corners to enclose the filling; continue to roll to the other end of the wrapper. Repeat with the remaining wrappers and filling.

Pour enough oil into a wok or deep-sided pan so that once the spring rolls are added, they can float. Heat to 160°C (325°F) and cook the spring rolls in batches of four for 3–4 minutes, or until golden brown. Drain on a wire rack or a plate lined with kitchen paper. Once all of the spring rolls are cooked, serve hot with Sweet Chilli Sauce.

SWEET LOTUS BAO

These Chinese steamed buns are light and fluffy, and stuffed with a sweet lotus paste (which can be bought in any Chinese supermarket). These would usually be served at the beginning of the meal as part of a dim sum menu to whet your appetite for the main courses, but to be honest, any time is a good time. Bao and tea in the morning; bao and coffee mid-morning; bao for lunch or even a bao and hot chocolate supper – simply delicious.

2½ HOURS　　**10 MINUTES**　　**MAKES 12**

560g (4¾ cups) plain (all-purpose) flour
11g (⅓oz) instant dried yeast
½ tsp salt
1 tsp baking powder
30g (1oz) caster (superfine) sugar
2 Tbsp vegetable oil
320ml (1¼ cups) whole milk (for a vegan option use soy or almond milk)
12 Tbsp lotus seed paste

For the dough, mix all of the ingredients, except the lotus paste, in a large bowl.

Turn out on to a clean lightly floured surface and knead for 6 minutes until the dough is soft, springy and not at all sticky. Bring the mixture together to form a ball, then place into a lightly greased bowl, cover and leave for 2 hours until the dough has doubled in size.

Turn out the dough on to a lightly floured work surface, lightly flatten and roll into a long sausage shape. Divide into 12 equal pieces and flatten each piece into a 12cm (5in) round.

Place 1 tablespoon of lotus paste into the centre of each bao and carefully bring the edges together to form a round parcel, twisting the top to form a seal. Repeat with the remaining dough.

Place the sealed dough balls on to a sheet of perforated baking paper in a bamboo steamer with a lid, leaving about 2cm (¾in) between each one as they will grow as they steam. Steam on high heat for 10 minutes. Be careful when you remove the lid as the escaping steam will billow around your hand. Remove from the basket and enjoy warm.

Note
You can also steam the bao without any filling – once you have cut the dough into equal pieces, simply roll into balls, place on non-stick paper and steam for 8–10 minutes.

TEMPURA VEG
WITH DIPPING SAUCE

The trick to crispy tempura batter is to fold, not whisk, and yes, lumps are absolutely fine. Follow these tips and you'll soon be enjoying amazingly light, crispy-covered vegetables, which can be served with your favourite dipping sauces. An appetiser that looks, feels and tastes delicious.

3-5 HOURS **10 MINUTES** **SERVES 3-4**

1 litre (4 cups) oil for deep-frying (ideally groundnut oil as it has a higher smoke point)

175g (1½ cups) plain (all-purpose) flour

1½ Tbsp cornflour (cornstarch)

¼ tsp baking powder

½ tsp salt

750ml (3 cups) iced water or ice-cold soda water

selection of your favourite vegetables cut into thin slices, such as courgette (zucchini), onion, pepper, carrot, sweet potato, baby corn

For the dipping sauce

2 sheets kombu seaweed flakes, crumbled

250ml (1 cup) water

4 Tbsp mirin

4 Tbsp light soy sauce

½ Tbsp sugar

To make the dipping sauce, add the crumbled kombu sheets to a bowl and pour over the water. Allow to steep for 3–5 hours, then remove the kombu pieces from the water, keeping the used kombu water to one side. Put the kombu water, mirin, soy sauce and sugar into a saucepan, bring to the boil and then turn off the heat and allow to cool. Transfer to a serving bowl.

Pour the oil for deep-frying into a large saucepan on a medium heat.

Combine the plain flour, cornflour, baking powder and salt in a large bowl. Pour in the water and use a fork to combine – it is perfectly fine to have small lumps of flour in your batter and it is important that you do not overwork the mixture, as this will build up the gluten in the flour and your batter will lose its lightness.

One at a time, dip the vegetables into the batter and then carefully lower into the oil, working in batches. Fry each vegetable for 3–5 minutes, turning them occasionally for even cooking and colour. Drain on kitchen paper and serve hot with your dipping sauce.

PANKO MUSHROOMS WITH OK DIPPING SAUCE

So, what's better than a mushroom starter? Mushrooms covered in a crispy panko crumb, of course. Crunchy on the outside and juicy on the inside, each mouthful is a taste sensation of juicy mushroom, oozing with garlic and cayenne pepper aromatics – and that's before you even get close to dipping into the silky, rich OK sauce.

10 MINUTES   **10 MINUTES**   **SERVES 3-4**

175ml (¾ cup) almond or soya milk
½ tsp garlic powder
¼ tsp cayenne pepper
½ Tbsp cornflour (cornstarch)
½ tsp salt
100g (¾ cup) plain (all-purpose) flour
125g (1 cup) panko breadcrumbs
200g (7oz) baby button mushrooms, wiped clean
250ml (1 cup) oil for shallow frying (vegetable, groundnut or coconut)

For the dipping sauce
2 tsp light soy sauce
1 tsp Chinese five spice
250ml (1 cup) water
125ml (½ cup) tomato ketchup
4 Tbsp brown table sauce
100g (½ cup) white or brown sugar
1½ tsp cornflour (cornstarch) mixed with 2 Tbsp water

Put all of the sauce ingredients except the cornflour mixture into a wok. Heat gently and stir until the sauce starts to boil. Lower the heat and simmer for a few minutes. Gradually add the cornflour mixture to the sauce, stirring constantly until thickened, then remove from the heat and set to one side.

In a large bowl, mix the almond or soya milk, garlic powder, cayenne pepper, cornflour and salt. Add the flour and mix gently to create a smooth, pouring consistency batter. Put the panko crumbs on to a large plate.

To assemble the mushrooms you'll need some surface space. Place the mushrooms on one side, with the batter in the middle, followed by the breadcrumbs. Dip each mushroom into the batter and then coat evenly with panko breadcrumbs, trying not to drip too much wet batter into the breadcrumbs. Heat enough oil to shallow fry in a large frying pan and fry the breaded mushrooms in batches over a medium heat for 2 minutes, or until golden brown. Transfer to a wire rack or kitchen paper to drain.

Serve the mushrooms with your OK dipping sauce.

SESAME SEED TEMPURA FRIED TOFU

Since around the eighth century, tofu has been much favoured by Zen Buddhist monks as a protein substitute for meat; over the centuries they have adapted and perfected recipes to create different textures. This recipe is one simple example of nutty sesame seeds in a crisp tempura batter enveloping firm yet creamy tofu.

25 MINUTES   **15 MINUTES**   **SERVES 2–3**

340g (12oz) firm tofu, cubed
85g (⅔ cup) plain (all-purpose) flour, plus extra for coating
½ tsp salt
½ tsp sugar
2 Tbsp sesame seeds
200ml (¾ cup) chilled sparkling water
1 litre (4 cups) groundnut oil for deep-frying

Pat the tofu pieces dry with kitchen paper and put to one side.

Put the flour, salt, sugar and sesame seeds into a large bowl and mix well. Using a balloon whisk, gradually stir in the sparkling water, it's ok to have small lumps of flour in the batter.

Place the oil in a large heavy-based saucepan over a medium heat.

Coat the tofu in flour, dust off any excess and then dip into the batter, allowing the excess to drip off. Carefully place the tofu into the hot oil and fry for 2–3 minutes until crispy and golden brown. Drain on a wire rack or kitchen paper. Serve with your favourite dipping sauce – Hoisin Sauce (page 154) for me please.

GRIDDLED SWEET POTATO PANCAKES

Served hot, warm or even cold, these ever-so-sweet pancakes are chewy, savoury and perfect at any time of the day. My own memories of these pancakes are when my auntie would bring over a batch for my dad and like any cheeky child I'd eagerly sneak a couple to savour in front of the TV.

1½ HOURS   **10 MINUTES**   **MAKES 12**

450g (1lb) sweet potatoes
70g (⅓ cup) sugar
220g (8oz) glutinous rice flour
2–3 Tbsp oil

Preheat the oven to 200°C (400°F). Bake the sweet potatoes in their skins in the oven for 1 hour, or until tender. Remove and allow to cool for 15 minutes.

Remove the skins from the sweet potatoes and set to one side, then place the flesh into a large bowl. Combine the flesh and sugar with a fork. Add the glutinous rice flour and knead together to create a dough. Divide the mixture into 12 equal-sized balls and then flatten each ball into a 10cm (4in) disc.

Pour the oil into a hot wok and gently fry the cakes for 2–3 minutes on each side until golden brown. Transfer to a wire rack or kitchen paper to drain.

Tip
Sprinkle the discarded skins with a little salt and Chinese five spice and lay out on a baking tray. Bake in the oven on a low heat until crisp. These are delicious snacks to be eaten with your favourite homemade Chinese dipping sauces.

TARO, SESAME & LOTUS PUK PUKS

Nothing quite compares to the taste or aroma of fried sesame seeds, and these little puk puks are smothered with them. Each disc is a combination of soft yet chewy, sweet yet savoury, and the nutty flavour of taro (a tropical root vegetable used extensively in Asian cuisine) makes this even better. My mouth is quite literally watering at the very thought of these delicious treats.

1 HOUR   **15 MINUTES**   **MAKES 12**

450g (1lb) taro
70g (⅓ cup) sugar
220g (8oz) glutinous rice flour
4 Tbsp lotus seed paste
140g (1 cup) sesame seeds
3 Tbsp oil (vegetable, groundnut or coconut)

Bring a large saucepan of water to the boil. Peel and cut the taro into thumb-sized chunks, then boil for 10–15 minutes, or until tender. Drain and allow to cool for 15 minutes.

Place the cooked taro into a large bowl and add the sugar, then mash with a fork and mix well. Add the glutinous rice flour and knead to create a dough. Divide the mixture into 12 equal-sized balls, then flatten each ball into a disc on a clean flat surface. Add 1 teaspoon of sweet lotus paste to the centre of each disc and gather up the sides to form a ball, enclosing the paste within the dough. Gently flatten each ball to make a circular shape.

Pour the sesame seeds on to a large plate and coat each puk evenly in the sesame seeds, pressing gently to ensure the seeds are sticking to the puks.

Heat the oil in a non-stick frying pan over a medium-high heat and fry each puk for 3 minutes on each side until golden brown and crispy. Transfer to a wire rack or kitchen paper to drain. Serve warm or cool.

LOTUS ROOT CRISPS

These crisps are absolutely stunning and guaranteed to create a talking point among friends, as they look fascinating and taste even better. Lotus root has also been noted for its many health benefits, including improving digestion, boosting the immune system and increasing blood circulation.

20 MINUTES   **10 MINUTES**   **SERVES 2-3**

340g (12oz) fresh lotus root
1 litre (4 cups) oil for frying
   (vegetable, groundnut or coconut)
½ Tbsp salt
½ Tbsp ground Sichuan pepper

Peel the lotus root and cut off both ends, then slice thinly, ideally with a mandolin to achieve really thin, even slices. Soak the slices in a large bowl of cold water for 5–10 minutes; this will not only stop the root from discolouring but will also help remove some of the excess starch.

Pour enough oil for deep-frying into a large saucepan on a medium heat. Meanwhile, drain the lotus root and rinse under cold water, then dry thoroughly on kitchen paper. Fry in small batches for 2–3 minutes, or until they turn a golden brown. It's very important not to over-fry these as lotus root can become bitter. Drain on kitchen paper.

Mix the salt and Sichuan pepper together and lightly sprinkle over the cooled lotus root crisps. Shake, serve and enjoy.

CAULIFLOWER YUK SUNG

Yuk Sung has been a favourite in Chinese restaurants and takeaways for many years. In this version, the crunchy cauliflower, soft onion and rich aromatic Cantonese sauce is served in a classic iceberg lettuce leaf and topped with crispy vermicelli and creamy cashew nuts.

30 MINUTES   **15 MINUTES**   **SERVES 3–4**

1 medium cauliflower
1½ Tbsp dark soy sauce
3 Tbsp Mushroom Stir-Fry Sauce (page 155 or use shop-bought)
1 Tbsp rice wine
1 Tbsp sugar
1 Tbsp groundnut oil, plus extra for shallow frying
2 garlic cloves, finely chopped
1 Tbsp grated fresh ginger
3 spring onions (scallions), thinly sliced
1 white onion, finely diced
1 large carrot, finely diced
2 celery sticks, finely diced
1 x 220g (8oz) can water chestnuts, drained and finely diced
1 Tbsp sesame oil
handful of vermicelli noodles
1 iceberg lettuce, separated into large leaves (see below)
40g (⅓ cup) roasted cashew nuts, roughly crushed

Cut the hard core and stalk from the cauliflower and separate into bite-sized florets.

In a small bowl, mix the soy sauce, Mushroom Stir-Fry Sauce, rice wine and sugar.

Gently heat the tablespoon of oil in a wok, add the garlic, ginger and spring onions and fry until aromatic. Add the cauliflower, onion, carrot, celery and water chestnuts and cook for 3–5 minutes, or until tender and browned. Add the soy sauce mixture and stir in well, continuing to cook over a high heat until the sauce has reduced. Once the mixture becomes quite dry, turn off the heat and drizzle with the sesame oil.

This next part is optional but highly recommended – it's fun to cook and delicious to eat, and used as a garnish as much as a texture addition. Heat 250ml (1 cup) of groundnut oil in a deep-sided frying pan, take a handful of vermicelli rice noodles and add them to the hot oil. They will puff up – FAST – so be ready to quickly push down any that are still transparent. Scoop them out as soon as they are puffed and white, and drain on kitchen paper before serving.

To serve, take a heaped spoonful of the cauliflower yuk sung and place in a lettuce leaf. Add a sprinkle of fried vermicelli and a pinch of crushed cashew nuts, wrap and eat.

Tip
Separate the lettuce leaves while trying to keep them intact. The best way to do this is to hold the lettuce under gently running cold water; as the leaves fill with water they peel (intact) away from the lettuce.

CAULIFLOWER FRITTERS

I love to eat certain foods with my hands; it adds to the experience, evokes emotion and arguably makes food *taste better*, and these little savoury fritters are no exception. Golden brown and crispy on the outside, succulent and tender on the inside and punching well above their weight on taste. Use chopsticks for a less messy experience!

30 MINUTES **15 MINUTES** **SERVES 3–4**

1 large head of cauliflower, cut into florets
1 large courgettes (zucchini), diced
60g (½ cup) plain (all-purpose) flour
2 eggs beaten (vegan option: use ½ cup silken tofu, blended smooth)
3 garlic cloves, finely chopped
1 Tbsp grated fresh ginger
1 tsp Chinese five spice
½ tsp salt
¼ tsp white pepper
3 Tbsp chopped spring onions (scallions)
2 Tbsp oil

Bring a large saucepan of water to the boil, add the cauliflower florets and cook for 2–3 minutes until tender. Drain and then cut into small pieces.

In a large bowl mix the cauliflower and courgettes with the flour, eggs (or tofu), garlic, ginger, Chinese five spice, salt, pepper and spring onions. Heat the oil in a large non-stick frying pan over a medium-high heat. Add scoops of the mixture to the hot oil, ensuring you leave enough room for them to spread during cooking. Cook for 2–3 minutes on each side until cooked through, crispy and golden brown. Transfer to kitchen paper to drain. Serve warm.

CHINESE BEER-BATTERED PAKODA

Who doesn't love fried finger food as a perfect weekend treat? Also known as Manchurian balls, these Indo-Chinese savoury bites are made using Chinese rice beer, which gives each pakoda a unique fermented rice flavour.

10 MINUTES   **15 MINUTES**   **SERVES 3-4**

150g (1¼ cups) buckwheat flour
75g (generous ½ cup) plain (all-purpose) flour
½ tsp chilli powder
1 tsp garlic powder
2 tsp onion powder
2 tsp Chinese five spice
½ tsp ground Sichuan pepper
¼ tsp baking powder
1 tsp salt
200ml (¾ cup) Chinese beer (Buddha or Tsing Tao)
180g (6oz) sweet potato, peeled and cut into small dice
1 onion, finely diced
1 green (bell) pepper, finely diced
5 spring onions (scallions), cut into thin rounds
1 tsp grated fresh ginger
1 litre (4 cups) oil (vegetable, groundnut or coconut) for deep-frying

In a large bowl, mix the flours, spices, baking powder and salt. Slowly pour in the beer, whisking the batter to a smooth, thick consistency. Stir in the sweet potato, onion, green pepper, spring onions and ginger.

Pour the oil for deep-frying into a large saucepan, adding enough oil to come no higher than a third of the way up the sides, and place over a medium-high heat. Working in batches of three or four fritters, drop spoonfuls of the mixture into the oil and fry for 5 minutes, or until golden brown, remembering to keep turning them as they cook to get an even colour. Drain on kitchen paper.

Serve with your favourite dipping sauce and a bottle of chilled Chinese beer.

MAINS

SPICY HOISIN MIXED VEGETABLES

Chunky vegetables stir-fried in a rich, sticky sweet, aromatic sauce, with a hint of chilli and served with creamy cashew nuts; it's no wonder that, once tried, this dish is cooked time and time again. Everything happens in your wok so washing up is a doddle afterwards too.

10 MINUTES   **5 MINUTES**   **SERVES 2**

1 Tbsp groundnut oil
4 garlic cloves, finely chopped
1 tsp grated fresh ginger
1 onion, diced
1 carrot, diced
30g (¼ cup) canned water chestnuts, drained
3 baby corn cobs, halved lengthways
35g (¼ cup) canned straw mushrooms, drained
60g (1 cup) button mushrooms, cut into bite-sized pieces
30g (¼ cup) canned bamboo shoots, drained
1 Tbsp rice vinegar
1 Tbsp soy sauce
½ cup Hoisin Sauce (page 154)
½ tsp dried chilli flakes
1 Tbsp cornflour (cornstarch) mixed with 2 Tbsp water
1 tsp sesame oil
30g (¼ cup) unsalted roasted cashew nuts (if you have salted cashew nuts, rinse under cold water and pat dry)

Place a wok over a medium-high heat. When hot, add the oil, garlic and ginger and fry until fragrant, about 15 seconds. Add the onion and carrot and fry for 2 minutes, then add the water chestnuts, baby corn, straw mushrooms, button mushrooms and bamboo shoots and stir-fry for a further 2 minutes. Turn the heat down to medium, add the rice vinegar, soy sauce, Hoisin Sauce and chilli flakes and stir-fry for a further 2–3 minutes.

Gradually add the cornflour mixture, stirring constantly to thicken the sauce. Remove from the heat, add the sesame oil and cashew nuts and mix well. Transfer to a serving dish and tuck in.

CRISPY TOFU WITH SPRING ONIONS

With just five basic ingredients, you really can create a dish that your family and friends will think you've spent days preparing. Aromatic spring onions and crispy tofu are served with a rich, tasty, fermented chilli bean sauce. This is traditional Chinese cooking at its simplest.

5 MINUTES   **10 MINUTES**   **SERVES 3-4**

340g (12oz) firm tofu
2 Tbsp groundnut oil
300g (10oz) spring onions (scallions),
   cut into 2.5cm (1in) lengths
2 tsp chilli bean paste
½ tsp sugar
1 tsp light soy sauce

Slice the tofu into 2cm (¾in) cubes and pat dry with kitchen paper. Heat a non-stick wok with half the oil and fry the tofu cubes until golden brown on all sides. Remove and drain on kitchen paper.

Heat the remaining oil in the wok over a medium heat, then add the spring onions and fry for 1 minute. Return the fried tofu to the pan with the chilli bean paste, sugar and soy sauce. Fry for a further 1–2 minutes and serve hot.

Tip
If you are able to buy pre-fried tofu you can use this instead of firm tofu, to make this recipe even speedier.

KUNG PO CAULIFLOWER

This is the spicy cousin of sweet and sour; you know the one...
cooler than you could ever imagine, the one that breaks all the
rules and not only gets away with it, but they are celebrated for it
too. Preparation is key to making this dish all it can be. You want to
serve this as fast as possible once the cauliflower comes out of the
fryer so that the light batter remains crispy as you chow down.

15 MINUTES   **25 MINUTES**   **SERVES 2–3**

1 head of cauliflower

50g (½ cup) cornflour (cornstarch)

1 egg, beaten (vegan option: use
¼ cup silken tofu blended until
completely smooth)

¼ tsp salt

groundnut oil for deep-frying, plus
1 tbsp

1 garlic clove, roughly crushed

½ small onion, roughly chopped

½ red (bell) pepper, roughly
chopped

30g (¼ cup) canned bamboo shoots,
drained and cut into small cubes

30g (¼ cup) canned water chestnuts,
drained and sliced

1 green bird's-eye chilli, finely
chopped

30g (¼ cup) roasted cashew nuts

For the kung po sauce

125ml (½ cup) water

2 Tbsp Hoisin Sauce (page 154)

2 Tbsp sugar

½ Tbsp tomato purée (paste)

1 Tbsp tomato ketchup

2 Tbsp rice vinegar

1 Tbsp cornflour (cornstarch) mixed
with 2 Tbsp water

For the sauce, place a large saucepan over a medium heat and
add the water, Hoisin Sauce, sugar, tomato purée, ketchup and rice
vinegar. Bring to the boil and then simmer for 5 minutes. Slowly
pour the cornflour mixture into the sauce, stirring continuously until
smooth enough to coat the back of a spoon – don't worry if you don't
need to use it all, thicken the sauce to your own personal preference.
Leave to one side.

Cut the hard core and stalk from the cauliflower and separate into
bite-sized florets. Coat each floret in cornflour then place into a
large bowl with the beaten egg, seasoned with the ¼ teaspoon of
salt (or use blended silken tofu) and gently fold through, coating
each piece thoroughly. On a separate plate, coat the dipped
cauliflower again with cornflour and tap off the excess.

In a deep-sided wok or saucepan heat enough oil for deep-frying to
180°C (350°F). Carefully drop the coated cauliflower florets into the
oil in batches and fry until crispy. Remove and drain on a wire rack
or kitchen paper.

Place a wok over a medium-high heat, add the tablespoon of oil and
fry the garlic for 15 seconds. Add the onion and red pepper and fry
for a further minute. Add the bamboo shoots, water chestnuts and
chilli and stir-fry for 1 minute more. Now add the prepared sauce
and reheat thoroughly, before turning off the heat and finally adding
the cooked cauliflower and cashew nuts. Stir gently to coat in the
sauce and transfer to a serving plate.

CHINESE ORANGE TOFU WITH PEPPERS & PINEAPPLE

Developed to cater for Western taste buds, this dish is a play on the much-loved and ever popular sweet and sour dish we see in all Chinese takeaways and restaurants. It's made with fresh orange juice, for a natural sweetness, zest for some twang, and a hint of garlic and ginger for that aromatic note. If you love sweet and sour, you're going to love this dish.

10 MINUTES   **15 MINUTES**   **SERVES 2**

500ml (2 cups) oil for shallow frying (vegetable, groundnut or coconut)
340g (12oz) firm tofu

For the sauce
1 Tbsp oil (vegetable, groundnut or coconut)
1 green (bell) pepper, roughly chopped
1 small carrot, cut into bite-sized slices
½ tsp grated fresh ginger
½ tsp grated garlic
1 tsp grated orange zest
250ml (1 cup) orange juice
2 Tbsp sugar
2 Tbsp tomato purée (paste)
3 Tbsp rice vinegar or white wine vinegar
handful of pineapple chunks
2 Tbsp cornflour (cornstarch) mixed with 4 Tbsp water

Heat the oil for shallow frying in a large saucepan to 180°C (350°F). The oil needs to be deep enough for the tofu to float without touching the bottom of the pan. Cut the tofu into bite-sized pieces and pat dry with kitchen paper, then gently add the tofu to the oil in batches and fry until golden brown. Drain on kitchen paper and set to one side.

Heat the oil for the sauce in a wok or frying pan and gently fry the green pepper and carrot over a medium-low heat until softened, then add the ginger, garlic and grated zest and fry until fragrant. Transfer to a bowl and set to one side.

Put the orange juice, sugar, tomato purée and rice vinegar into a large saucepan and place over a medium heat. Bring to the boil, then add the softened vegetables along with the pineapple and allow to simmer for a further 5 minutes. Give the cornflour mixture a stir and slowly pour into the sauce, a little at a time, stirring constantly until you have the desired consistency. Stir the tofu through the sauce to gently reheat and serve immediately.

SICHUAN PEPPER MUSHROOMS

These mushrooms are packed full of wondrous flavour as they are infused with the holy trinity of Cantonese cooking – garlic, ginger and spring onion – but this recipe also borrows ingredients from the Sichuan province. The taste is often described as aromatic, pungent (from the rice wine) and mouth-numbingly spicy.

10 MINUTES   **20 MINUTES**   **SERVES 2-3**

1 tsp Sichuan peppercorns
1 Tbsp vegetable oil
2 garlic cloves, finely chopped
1 Tbsp grated fresh ginger
2 spring onions (scallions), thinly sliced
2 large dried chillies, thinly sliced
1 onion, thinly sliced
3 large portobello mushrooms, quartered (they will shrink when cooked)
125ml (½ cup) Chinese rice wine
500ml (2 cups) vegetable stock
2 Tbsp soy sauce

Place the Sichuan peppercorns in a dry wok or heavy-based frying pan over a medium-low heat. Heat the peppercorns, shaking the pan occasionally until they begin to darken and become fragrant, then set aside to cool. When cooled, lightly bruise (not crush) the toasted peppercorns using a mortar and pestle or rolling pin.

Heat the oil in a wok, add the garlic, ginger and spring onions and fry until fragrant. Add the Sichuan peppercorns and dried chillies and stir for 20 seconds, then add the onion and mushrooms and fry for a further 1 minute. Pour in the rice wine and cook until the liquor has been absorbed. Add the vegetable stock and soy sauce and bring to the boil, then turn down to a medium heat and simmer for 10–15 minutes, or until the mushrooms are tender and the sauce is syrupy (keep an eye on the pan, to avoid burning the sauce). Stir and serve.

CHINESE MUSHROOM CURRY

I'm pretty sure that most of you have tried the classic Chinese curry sauce and this leaves me with a dilemma: I'm fully aware that you already know what it 'should' taste like... Well I can confidently tell you that this recipe is bulletproof – you'll be pleasantly surprised at just how simple it is to knock up your own batch at home.

5 MINUTES   **25 MINUTES**   **SERVES 2**

1 Tbsp oil (vegetable, groundnut or coconut)
1 onion, diced
300g (10oz) mushrooms (use your favourite), cut into bite-sized pieces
¼ tsp salt
¼ tsp sugar
30g (¼ cup) peas

For the sauce
1 Tbsp oil (vegetable, groundnut or coconut)
2 onions, finely diced
5 garlic cloves, finely chopped
2 carrots, finely diced
1 celery stick, finely diced
2 Tbsp plain (all-purpose) flour
1½ Tbsp curry powder (use your favourite: mild, medium or hot)
600ml (2½ cups) vegetable stock
½ Tbsp honey
1½ Tbsp soy sauce
1 bay leaf
1 tsp garam masala

For the sauce, heat the oil in a saucepan, then add the onions and garlic and cook until softened. Stir in the carrots and celery and cook over a low heat for 10–12 minutes. Add the flour and curry powder and cook for 1 minute. Gradually pour in the stock, stirring constantly until combined, then add the honey, soy sauce and bay leaf. Slowly bring to the boil. Simmer for 15 minutes, or until the sauce thickens but is still of pouring consistency. If your sauce is too thick, add a splash of water to loosen it. Stir in the garam masala, then strain the curry sauce through a sieve and set to one side.

Place a wok over a medium heat and add the oil. Once the oil is hot, add the onion and mushrooms and stir-fry for 2–3 minutes until the onions have softened. Add the salt and sugar, mix well and then pour in the curry sauce and peas. Bring the sauce back to the boil, then reduce the heat and simmer for 3 minutes, allowing the curry sauce to thicken again. Transfer to a bowl and serve.

CHILLI SALT TOFU

By dipping the tofu first in cornflour and then frying it, you're able to achieve a light, crisp coating that absorbs the flavours of the fried garlic, onion and pepper as you toss the ingredients together in your searing hot wok. Follow up with a fine dusting of Chinese five spice, salt and pepper and you're well on your way to creating a seriously great-tasting plate of food.

10 MINUTES   **10 MINUTES**   **SERVES 2**

340g (12oz) firm tofu
50g (½ cup) cornflour (cornstarch)
1 egg, beaten (vegan option: use ¼ cup silken tofu blended until completely smooth)
½ Tbsp salt
½ Tbsp Chinese five spice
1 tsp black pepper
250ml (1 cup) oil for shallow frying (vegetable, groundnut or coconut), plus 1 Tbsp
1 small white onion, finely chopped
½ green (bell) pepper, finely chopped
2 green bird's-eye chillies, finely chopped
1 garlic clove, finely chopped
1 tsp sesame oil

Cut the tofu into 2cm (¾in) cubes and pat dry on kitchen paper. Coat in cornflour then place into a large bowl with the beaten egg or blended silken tofu and gently fold through, coating each piece. Coat the dipped tofu again with cornflour and tap off any excess.

In a separate bowl mix the salt, Chinese five spice and black pepper together and set aside.

In a high-sided wok or deep saucepan heat enough oil to shallow fry the tofu to 180°C (350°F). Gently lower the tofu into the oil and fry for about 3 minutes, turning once or twice to allow each piece to brown evenly. Remove from the oil and place on a wire rack or kitchen paper to drain.

Heat the tablespoon of oil in a wok or frying pan and wait until the oil just begins to smoke. Add the onion, green pepper and chillies and stir-fry for 30 seconds over a high heat, then add the garlic and stir through. Add the fried tofu and evenly sprinkle in the five spice mixture, quickly tossing the ingredients to coat each piece. Turn off the heat, drizzle with sesame oil and serve immediately.

CAULIFLOWER STEAK WITH A RICH CHINESE GRAVY

I love a big pile of rice smothered in gravy; for me it is comfort on a plate. This recipe is quite simply, 'food for your soul'. A huge Cantonese marinated cauliflower steak that is juicy on the inside and deliciously crispy on the outside, smothered in a rich dark aromatic gravy – it's a win-win dish.

10 MINUTES   **25 MINUTES**   **SERVES 3-4**

½ tsp salt
½ tsp black pepper
½ tsp garlic powder
½ tsp onion powder
½ tsp Chinese five spice
1 large head of cauliflower
2 Tbsp groundnut oil
2 tsp sesame oil

For the gravy
2 Tbsp Mushroom Stir-Fry Sauce
  (page 155 or use shop-bought)
1 Tbsp rice wine
1 tsp dark soy sauce
pinch of white pepper
250ml (1 cup) vegetable stock
1 tsp cornflour (cornstarch)
1 tsp groundnut oil
2 garlic cloves, roughly chopped

Preheat the oven to 200°C (400°F). Combine the salt, black pepper, garlic powder, onion powder and Chinese five spice in a large bowl and set aside.

Remove the outer leaves and tough stalk from the cauliflower, then slice the head into 4cm (1½in) thick steaks. Rub groundnut oil into both sides of the cauliflower steak and sprinkle liberally with the seasoning mixture, then place the steaks on a lined baking sheet and tightly cover with foil. Bake in the oven for 8 minutes, then remove the foil and continue to roast for a further 8 minutes.

While the cauliflower is roasting make the gravy: combine the stir-fry sauce, rice wine, dark soy sauce, white pepper, vegetable stock and cornflour in a bowl and mix well. Heat a wok over a medium-high heat. Add the oil and fry the garlic until fragrant, then add the stock mixture and bring to the boil. Turn down to simmer for 2 minutes, then remove from the heat and set aside.

Remove the roasted cauliflower from the oven and transfer to a hot frying pan. Fry the cauliflower steaks on both sides to form a rich, dark golden crust. Transfer to your serving plate, drizzle with the sesame oil and pour over the gravy.

KATSU CAULIFLOWER WITH TONKATSU SAUCE

Panko breadcrumbs are super crispy even before you fry them and they bring a crunch to a dish that standard breadcrumbs just can't deliver. As you cut into this cauliflower steak you'll instantly release the aromatics; as they waft up your nose and trigger your taste buds, this is when your mouth will begin to water uncontrollably. Then you dip into the rich, sweet and sour BBQ sauce and it's game over.

20 MINUTES   **20 MINUTES**   **SERVES 2-3**

1 large head of cauliflower
200ml (¾ cup) almond or soya milk
½ tsp garlic powder
½ tsp onion powder
½ Tbsp cornflour (cornstarch)
½ tsp salt
100g (¾ cup) plain (all-purpose) flour
100g (2 cups) panko breadcrumbs
oil for shallow frying (vegetable, groundnut or coconut)

For the sauce
1 Tbsp light soy sauce
¼ tsp garlic powder
100ml (½ cup) tomato ketchup
3 Tbsp Worcestershire sauce
2 Tbsp white or brown sugar

In a large bowl, mix together all of the sauce ingredients.

Remove the outer leaves and stalk from the cauliflower, then slice the head into 4cm (1½in) thick steaks. In a large bowl, mix together the almond or soya milk, garlic powder, onion powder, cornflour, salt and plain flour and mix well to create a smooth, pouring consistency batter. Spread out the panko breadcrumbs on a large plate. Dip the cauliflower steaks into the batter and then coat with panko breadcrumbs, pressing down to ensure the crumbs stick.

Pour enough oil to deep-fry the cauliflower steaks into a large saucepan and heat to 170°C (340°F). Carefully lower in the cauliflower steaks and fry for 5 minutes on each side, or until tender and golden brown. Transfer to a wire rack or kitchen paper to drain.

Slice each steak into slices and serve with the Tonkatsu sauce.

TERIYAKI BOWL

Sometimes all we want is a big bowl of love; something simple to make that isn't going to create an explosion of pots and pans to wash up afterwards. A mountain of yummy vegetables in a rich, aromatic, velvety umami sweet chilli sauce, served over noodles or steamed rice, is just the ticket for moments like these.

10 MINUTES   **10 MINUTES**   **SERVES 2**

1 Tbsp oil
1 onion, roughly diced
1 tsp grated garlic
2 tsp grated fresh ginger
1 red (bell) pepper, roughly diced
1 courgette (zucchini), cut into
  bite-sized pieces
60g (2oz) long-stem broccoli,
  cut into small florets
6–8 baby corn cobs
1 medium aubergine (eggplant),
  cut into bite-sized pieces

For the sauce
125ml (½ cup) light soy sauce
3 Tbsp brown sugar
2 tsp dried chilli flakes
1 Tbsp honey (vegan option: use
  agave or maple syrup)

Combine all of the sauce ingredients in a bowl, mix well and set to one side.

Heat the oil in a wok over a medium-high heat, add the onion, garlic and ginger and fry until fragrant and the onion is translucent. Add the remaining vegetables and stir-fry for 3–4 minutes. Add the sauce mixture, bring to the boil and simmer for 3 minutes.

Serve on top of freshly steamed rice or springy noodles.

HOISIN-GLAZED TEMPEH

Tempeh has an amazing texture; it's much firmer than tofu as it's made using the entire soya bean. Once fried, the tempeh becomes crispy and when added to a sauce it absorbs it like a sponge. The rich hoisin sauce is perfect for this dish – the tempeh becomes sweet, savoury and spicy with a crisp outside, but then give it a sprinkle of sesame seeds and the flavour dimensions really soar.

5 MINUTES   **10 MINUTES**   **SERVES 2–3**

1 x 340g (12oz) block of tempeh
3 Tbsp oil
2 garlic cloves, finely chopped
1 Tbsp grated fresh ginger
75ml (⅓ cup) Hoisin Sauce
  (page 154 or use shop-bought)
1 tsp sesame oil
1 Tbsp toasted sesame seeds
2 spring onions (scallions), thinly
  sliced

Cut the tempeh into bite-sized pieces and pat dry on kitchen paper.

Heat 2 tablespoons of the oil in a non-stick frying pan over a medium-high heat and fry the tempeh until golden brown on all sides. Transfer to kitchen paper to drain.

Heat your wok over a medium-high heat and add the remaining tablespoon of oil along with the garlic and ginger, cooking for 20–30 seconds until fragrant. Add the cooked tempeh and Hoisin Sauce and stir-fry for 3 minutes. Transfer to a serving bowl, drizzle with the sesame oil and sprinkle with the toasted sesame seeds and the sliced spring onions.

MAPO TOFU

Having been eaten for centuries in China, this dish is finally getting its much deserved recognition in Western countries. The soft tofu along with the mouth-numbing heat of the Sichuan peppercorns is something quite special to experience; combined with the fermented tang of the chilli bean sauce and the smooth silky sensation from the dashi, this is a dish to really wow friends and family.

5 MINUTES **25 MINUTES** **SERVES 2**

2 tsp Sichuan peppercorns, bruised in a pestle and mortar (or use the back of a spoon)
2 Tbsp oil (vegetable, groundnut or coconut)
150g (5oz) mushrooms, diced
1 onion, finely diced
2 Tbsp grated fresh ginger
5 garlic cloves, finely chopped
½ tsp Chinese five spice
2 Tbsp rice wine
3 Tbsp chilli bean sauce
1 Tbsp chilli oil
½ Tbsp light soy sauce
½ Tbsp dark soy sauce
250ml (1 cup) dashi stock
200g (7oz) silken tofu, cut into bite-sized cubes
2 spring onions (scallions), sliced (optional)

Gently toast the bruised Sichuan peppercorns for 1–2 minutes in a dry wok over a medium heat. Transfer to a bowl.

Place the wok over a medium-high heat and add the oil and then the mushrooms and fry until all of the mushroom liquid has evaporated. Add the onion, ginger and garlic and fry for a further 1 minute.

Add the toasted Sichuan peppercorns and five spice and continue to fry for 1 more minute. Add the rice wine, followed by the chilli bean sauce, chilli oil and light and dark soy sauces and mix well, then stir in the stock. Bring the sauce to the boil and then turn down to simmer for 10 minutes, or until the sauce has reduced by one-third and thickened. Finally add the tofu cubes and gently fold through the sauce. Transfer to a plate, sprinkle with the sliced spring onions and serve.

PURPLE SPROUTING BROCCOLI & PEANUT SATAY SAUCE

Satay sauce varies from region to region; it originates from Indonesia but was widely adopted by the Chinese for their love of peanuts – this sauce has lots of them. Young tender broccoli stems are lightly steamed and smothered in a rich, spicy–sour peanut sauce. Delicious simplicity on your plate.

5 MINUTES   **10 MINUTES**   **SERVES 2–3**

1 Tbsp sesame seeds, toasted
3 Tbsp chunky peanut butter
1 Tbsp rice vinegar
2 Tbsp light soy sauce
1 tsp chilli flakes (optional)
280g (9oz) purple sprouting broccoli

Toast the sesame seeds in a dry frying pan or wok over a medium heat until lightly golden and fragrant. Combine the peanut butter, vinegar, soy sauce and chilli flakes (if using) in a small saucepan over a low heat, stirring until warmed and completely combined.

Trim the broccoli stems and cut them into bite-sized pieces, then place in a steamer basket and steam for 4–5 minutes, or until tender. Remove the broccoli from the steamer and arrange on a serving plate, then pour over the satay sauce and sprinkle with the toasted sesame seeds.

STIR-FRIED AUBERGINE WITH SESAME SEEDS

Toasted sesame seeds always add an extra special something to a dish; not only do they offer little nibbles of crunch, they also pack a punch of distinctly nutty flavour that is totally unique to these tiny morsels. Here we have soft aubergine stir-fried in a rich, dark, aromatic sauce with a subtle sour note and rich umami taste, amped to the next level by a liberal sprinkling of sesame seeds.

10 MINUTES   **15 MINUTES**   **SERVES 2-3**

2 Tbsp sesame seeds
1 Tbsp light soy sauce
½ Tbsp dark soy sauce
1 Tbsp rice vinegar
1 Tbsp rice wine
½ Tbsp sugar
1 tsp cornflour (cornstarch)
2 Tbsp oil
2 garlic cloves, roughly chopped
1 Tbsp grated fresh ginger
2 spring onions (scallions), halved and thinly sliced lengthways
1 green bird's-eye chilli, thinly sliced
2 large aubergines (eggplants), cut into bite-sized pieces
4 Tbsp water
1 tsp sesame oil

Heat a dry, non-stick pan over a medium-high heat and toast the sesame seeds until lightly browned and fragrant. Transfer to a bowl and set to one side. In a bowl combine the light and dark soy sauces, rice vinegar, rice wine, sugar and cornflour and mix well. Set to one side.

Heat a wok over a medium-high heat and add the oil, garlic, ginger and spring onions and fry for 30 seconds until fragrant. Add the chilli and fry for a further 30 seconds before adding the aubergine and frying for 1 minute more. Add the water and turn the heat down to a simmer. After 10 minutes of simmering time, increase the heat, add the soy sauce mixture and combine well. Continue cooking over a medium-high heat to reduce the liquid by half.

Transfer to a serving plate, drizzle with the sesame oil and sprinkle with the toasted sesame seeds.

BOK CHOY WITH MUSHROOM STIR-FRY SAUCE

Bok Choy (also known as pak choi) literally translates as 'small white vegetable'. This type of Chinese cabbage, with its dark leaves and bulbous white bottom or stem, is used extensively in Cantonese and Chinese cookery. This simple dish cooks in minutes and delivers a clean, fresh, aromatic taste.

5 MINUTES   **6 MINUTES**   **SERVES 2**

400g (14oz) bok choy
2 Tbsp groundnut oil
1 tsp grated fresh ginger
1 garlic clove, roughly chopped
1 Tbsp rice wine
3 Tbsp Mushroom Stir-Fry Sauce
   (page 155 or use shop-bought)
1 tsp sesame oil

Rinse the bok choy and cut lengthways into quarters.

Heat a wok over a medium-high heat and add the oil, then the ginger and garlic, frying for 30 seconds until fragrant. Add the quartered bok choy and stir-fry for 2 minutes, before adding the rice wine and cooking for a further 2 minutes. Add the Mushroom Stir-Fry Sauce, mix well and transfer the saucy bok choy to a plate. Drizzle with the sesame oil and serve.

MOCK CHAR SIU BAO WITH PICKLED CHINESE VEGETABLES

Soft, fluffy steamed buns – check. Firm tempeh patty filling, marinated in a rich, aromatically smoky, sweet Chinese barbecue sauce – check. Topping of tangy, sour, crunchy, pickled vegetables – check. A combination that will no doubt get your taste buds tingling.

2 HRS 20 MINS **20 MINUTES** **SERVES 4**

For the bao
560g (4¾ cups) plain (all-purpose) flour
11g (⅓oz) instant dried yeast
½ tsp salt
1 tsp baking powder
30g (1oz) caster (superfine) sugar
2 Tbsp vegetable oil
320ml (1¼ cups) whole milk (for a vegan option use soy or almond milk)

For the filling
125ml (½ cup) hoisin sauce (page 90 or use shop-bought)
1 Tbsp Chinese five spice
1 Tbsp rice wine
2 Tbsp sugar
1 Tbsp oil
1 x 340g (12oz) block of tempeh, cut into 2cm (¾in) thick patties

4 Tbsp Chinese Pickled Vegetables (page 152)

Put all of the bao ingredients into a large bowl and bring together to form a soft and springy dough. Turn out on to a clean lightly floured work surface and knead for 6 minutes, then bring the mixture together to form a ball. Place in a lightly greased bowl, cover and leave to stand for 2 hours, or until the dough has doubled in size.

Turn out the dough on to a lightly floured work surface, lightly flatten and roll into a long sausage shape, then divide into 8–12 equal pieces (depending on how large you'd like your bao to be). Roll each piece into a short sausage shape and flatten, then fold in half to create a soft clam shape. Place the sealed dough balls on to a sheet of perforated baking paper in a bamboo steamer with a lid, leaving about 2cm (¾in) between each one as they will grow as they steam. Steam on high heat for 8–10 minutes. Be careful when you remove the lid as the escaping steam will billow around your hand. Remove from the basket and enjoy warm.

Meanwhile, for the filling, preheat the oven to 190°C (375°F). Combine the hoisin sauce, Chinese five spice, rice wine and sugar in a large bowl.

Line a baking sheet with foil and brush with the oil, then place the tempeh patties on to the foil and brush over half of the marinade. Bake in the oven for 10 minutes, or until they have formed a crust, then turn the patties over, brush on the remainder of the marinade and cook for a further 10 minutes.

Take a steamed bao and carefully pull it open (you may need to cut it with a knife). Place a tempeh patty in the middle, top with some pickled vegetables and tuck in.

FRIED TOFU WITH CHILLI & BLACK BEANS

Few dishes pack a punch on flavour like this one; not only do you get the texture of crispy fried tofu, crunchy green peppers and soft onion, but you also get the pungent taste explosion of salty, spicy, umami and aromatic. A seriously popular and tasty dish.

10 MINUTES　　**10 MINUTES**　　**SERVES 2–3**

340g (12oz) firm tofu
2 Tbsp groundnut oil
1 white onion, chopped into 2cm (¾in) cubes
1 green bird's-eye chilli (optional)
2 tsp grated fresh ginger
1 garlic clove, finely chopped
1 green (bell) pepper, chopped into 2cm (¾in) cubes
1 carrot, cut into matchsticks
3 Tbsp Chinese fermented black beans
1 Tbsp light soy sauce
1 Tbsp dark soy sauce
½ tsp salt (or to taste)
½ tsp sugar
½ tsp white pepper
125ml (½ cup) vegetable stock
1 Tbsp cornflour (cornstarch) mixed with 2 Tbsp water
1 tsp sesame oil

Chop the tofu into bite-sized pieces and pat dry with kitchen paper. Heat a non-stick wok or frying pan with half the oil, add the tofu to the pan and fry until golden brown on all sides. Remove and drain on kitchen paper.

Add the remaining tablespoon of oil to the wok or pan and place over a medium heat. Add the onion, chilli (if using), ginger and garlic and stir-fry for 1 minute, or until the onions become translucent. Now add the green pepper, carrot, the fried tofu and the black beans and stir-fry for a further 2 minutes.

Add the light and dark soy sauces, salt, sugar, white pepper and vegetable stock to the wok or pan, combine well and bring to the boil. Slowly pour in the cornflour mixture, stirring constantly until the sauce is thickened to the desired consistency. Remove from the heat, stir in the sesame oil and serve.

SICHUAN CRISP CAULIFLOWER

Succulent pieces of cauliflower covered in a crispy coating and drenched in a rich velvety sauce that is sweet, a little sour, spicy, pleasantly aromatic and silky smooth, thanks to a glug of dark soy sauce. There's so much happening in this dish that your taste buds are going to party for quite a while after you devour each mouthful.

10 MINUTES   **15 MINUTES**   **SERVES 2**

1 head of cauliflower
50g (½ cup) cornflour (cornstarch)
1 Tbsp garlic salt
1 Tbsp Chinese five spice
1 egg, beaten (vegan option: use ¼ cup silken tofu blended until completely smooth)
groundnut oil for deep-frying, plus 1 Tbsp
2 garlic cloves, roughly chopped
8 whole dried red chillies
½ Tbsp grated fresh ginger
1 onion, sliced
½ tsp salt
½ tsp ground black pepper

For the sauce
1 Tbsp dried chilli flakes
2 garlic cloves, finely chopped
1 Tbsp light soy sauce
½ Tbsp dark soy sauce
1 tsp Chinese black vinegar (or use a good balsamic vinegar)
2 tsp cornflour (cornstarch)
75ml (⅓ cup) vegetable stock

Place a large saucepan over a medium heat and add all the sauce ingredients. Bring to the boil and then simmer for 2 minutes. Remove from the heat and set aside.

Cut the hard core and stalk from the cauliflower and separate the head into bite-sized florets. In a large bowl combine the cornflour, garlic salt and Chinese five spice. Coat each floret in the cornflour mixture then place into a large bowl with the beaten egg or blended silken tofu and gently fold through, coating each piece thoroughly. Cover the coated cauliflower with more of the cornflour mixture and dust off any excess.

Heat enough oil to deep-fry the cauliflower in a large saucepan to 180°C (350°F). Carefully drop the cauliflower florets into the oil in batches and fry until crisp. Remove and drain on a wire rack or kitchen paper.

Place a wok over a medium-high heat, add the tablespoon of oil along with the garlic, dried red chillies and ginger and fry for 20 seconds until fragrant. Add the onion, salt and black pepper and fry for a further minute, then add the prepared sauce and simmer until thickened. Turn off the heat, add the crispy cauliflower and toss to combine.

BLACK PEPPER TEMPEH WITH GREEN PEPPERS & ONIONS

Tempeh is a great alternative to tofu; it's much firmer as it uses the whole soya bean, which means it retains a higher protein and fibre content. It's the perfect ingredient for this dish as the tempeh naturally absorbs the flavours it's cooked with. The black pepper imbues this dish with a smoky, peppery taste, while the garlic and ginger bring home the Cantonese aromatics.

10 MINUTES   **5 MINUTES**   **SERVES 2–3**

2 tsp whole black peppercorns
2 Tbsp Mushroom Stir-Fry Sauce (page 155 or use shop-bought)
1 Tbsp Chinese rice wine
2 tsp light soy sauce
150ml (⅔ cup) vegetable stock
1½ Tbsp groundnut oil
1 onion, cut into 2cm (¾in) squares
2 garlic cloves, thinly sliced
½ Tbsp grated fresh ginger
1 x 340g (12oz) block of tempeh, cut into bite-sized pieces
1 green (bell) pepper, cut into 2cm (¾in) squares
1 Tbsp cornflour (cornstarch) mixed with 2 Tbsp of water
2 spring onions (scallions), thinly sliced
1 tsp sesame oil

Coarsely grind the peppercorns in a pestle and mortar – not too finely but you don't want any whole peppercorns either.

Combine the Mushroom Stir-Fry Sauce, rice wine, soy sauce and stock in a bowl and set to one side.

Heat your wok over a high heat. Once the wok starts to smoke immediately add the oil, onion, garlic and ginger. Cook until fragrant and the onions are translucent, then add the tempeh and green pepper. Fry for a further 1–2 minutes, then add the crushed black peppercorns and mix well for 1 minute. Add the stock mixture and bring to the boil; once boiling, give the cornflour mixture a stir and slowly drizzle into the sauce, stirring continuously until the sauce thickens.

Transfer immediately to a serving plate and sprinkle with the spring onions and a drizzle of sesame oil.

CRISPY CHILLI CAULIFLOWER

Picture this: golden nuggets of crispy coated cauliflower smothered in a sticky, garlicky, aromatic and very sweet yet sour sauce with crunchy carrot batons and soft translucent onions. I dare you to try this dish – it may just change your life.

10 MINUTES · **15 MINUTES** · **SERVES 2–3**

1 head of cauliflower
50g (½ cup) cornflour (cornstarch)
1 egg, beaten (vegan option: use ¼ cup of silken tofu blended until completely smooth)
groundnut oil for deep-frying, plus 1 tbsp
2 Tbsp grated fresh ginger
2 spring onions (scallions), thinly sliced
4 garlic cloves, finely chopped
1 carrot, cut into thick matchsticks
½ white onion, sliced
3 Tbsp soy sauce
4 Tbsp rice vinegar
1 Tbsp sugar
2 Tbsp honey
3 tsp dried chilli flakes
½ Tbsp sesame oil

Remove the hard core and stalk from the cauliflower and divide the head into bite-sized florets. Coat each floret in cornflour then place into a large bowl with the beaten egg (or tofu) and gently fold through, coating each piece. Cover the cauliflower with more cornflour and dust off any excess.

Pour enough oil into a large saucepan to deep-fry the cauliflower and heat to 180°C (350°F). Carefully drop the dipped cauliflower into the oil in batches and fry until crispy. Remove and drain on a wire rack or kitchen paper.

Heat the tablespoon of oil in a wok, add the ginger, spring onions and garlic and fry for about 30 seconds until fragrant. Add the carrot and onion and continue to fry for a further 1 minute. Transfer to a plate and set aside.

Wipe out the wok and return to a medium-high heat. Add the soy sauce, rice vinegar, sugar, honey and chilli flakes, bringing the mixture to a boil. Turn down to a simmer and allow to reduce by a third. Add the carrot and onion mixture and gently fold in the crispy cauliflower florets to coat in the sauce. Drizzle with the sesame oil. Serve and enjoy.

RICE

OVEN STEAMED RICE

No stirring, no pot watching – the only thing you need to do is keep an eye on the time.

2 MINUTES   **25 MINUTES**   **SERVES 2**

180g (1 cup) long-grain rice
500ml (2 cups) water

Preheat the oven to 170°C (340°F).

Wash the rice under warm water to remove the excess starch, then drain and tip into an ovenproof dish. Add the measured water, cover with a lid and bake for 25 minutes, or until the water has been fully absorbed. Remove from the oven, fluff up the cooked rice and serve with your favourite vegetable dish.

JASMINE RICE

These long-grain rice kernels have a fragrance reminiscent of jasmine and popcorn. Jasmine rice is slightly sweeter in taste than traditional long-grain rice, and stickier, so the grains will cling together.

5 MINUTES   **25 MINUTES**   **SERVES 4**

360g (2 cups) jasmine rice
1 tsp salt

Put the rice into a medium saucepan and fill with warm water. Rubbing your hands together, wash the rice in the pan, then carefully drain away the water. Repeat this process at least three times as this helps to remove some of the starch. Cover the washed rice with cold water so the water level sits 2.5cm (1in) above the rice, then add the salt. Place over a high heat and bring to the boil – it is important you **do not** stir and you must give your full attention to the pan. As soon as the water has been absorbed and tiny craters appear in the rice, turn the heat down to its lowest setting and place the lid firmly on to the saucepan (sealing in the steam). Leave for 2 minutes and then switch off the heat – don't be tempted to remove the lid (no peeking) as you want to keep the steam in the pan. Leave to steam in the residual heat for a further 10 minutes.

Remove the lid and stir the rice with a spoon to loosen the grains. Serve your perfect fluffy jasmine rice immediately.

COCONUT RICE

This creamy, sticky rice can be served as a dish all on its own; it's packed full of flavour with Cantonese aromatics and the rich creamy taste of coconut. It's also a fantastic side dish to any sweet recipe as the creamy flavour cuts through the sweetness, balancing the entire meal. I like it with Crispy Chilli Cauliflower (page 95), but I'll leave it up to you.

5 MINUTES   **25 MINUTES**   **SERVES 4**

360g (2 cups) long-grain rice
½ Tbsp oil (vegetable, groundnut or coconut)
1 small onion, finely diced
1 garlic clove, finely chopped
500ml (2 cups) coconut milk
500ml (2 cups) vegetable stock (this may vary depending on the size of your saucepan)

Wash the rice under warm water to remove the excess starch, then drain and set to one side.

Heat the oil in a medium saucepan and fry the onion and garlic for 2 minutes. Turn the heat down to low and add the washed rice, stirring until it is all mixed through. Add the coconut milk and enough of the vegetable stock so that the top of the liquid sits 2.5cm (1in) above the top of the rice. Increase the heat to high and bring to the boil – it is important you **do not** stir. As soon as the liquid has been absorbed and tiny craters appear in the rice, turn the heat down to its lowest setting and place the lid firmly on to the saucepan (sealing in the steam). Leave for 2 minutes and then switch off the heat – don't be tempted to remove the lid, not even for a sneaky peek. Leave to steam in the residual heat for a further 10 minutes.

Serve alone or accompanied – let your taste buds decide.

EIGHT TREASURE FRIED RICE

Since the Western Zhou dynasty in ancient China, around 2,000 years ago, eight treasure fried rice has been traditionally served during Chinese New Year. 'Why eight?' I hear you ask? Well, in China the word for eight is *ba* which sounds like *fa*, which means fortune.

5 MINUTES   **10 MINUTES**   **SERVES 2**

1½ Tbsp oil (vegetable, groundnut or coconut)
1 small onion, diced
1 small carrot, diced
30g (¼ cup) canned bamboo shoots, drained and sliced
35g (¼ cup) canned straw mushrooms, drained
½ red (bell) pepper, diced
¼ cup canned sweetcorn
30g (¼ cup) peas
250g (9oz) cooked steamed rice, cold (page 98 or use pre-cooked packets of rice)
3 spring onions (scallions), sliced, plus extra for serving
1 Tbsp light soy sauce
½ Tbsp dark soy sauce
2 Tbsp Mushroom Stir-Fry Sauce (page 155 or use shop-bought)
salt to taste
1 tsp sesame oil

Pour the oil into a wok and place over a medium–high heat, then add the onion and carrot and stir-fry for 1 minute. Add the remaining vegetables and cook for a further 1–2 minutes, or until any liquid has been evaporated.

Add the rice and cook for 2–3 minutes – remember, this is **fried** rice so your wok needs to be hot, hot, hot and you should be able to hear the ingredients sizzling as you cook. Add the light and dark soy sauces, Mushroom Stir-Fry Sauce and salt to taste. Continue frying until the rice is completely heated through and is piping hot. Remove from the heat, stir in the sesame oil, sprinkle with spring onions, serve and enjoy.

STICKY RICE PARCELS

Glutinous rice, wrapped in a lotus leaf and bursting with marinated trinkets of yumminess. Dating back to the time when weary travellers made the journey along the Old Silk Road, small resting houses, or tea houses, were established, offering refreshments and sustenance. In Chinese they were referred to as yum cha houses, translated as 'the act of drinking tea'.

2½ HOURS   **1½ HOURS**   **SERVES 2–4**

360g (2 cups) glutinous rice
2–3 dried lotus leaves
3 tsp vegetable oil
1 whole shallot, finely diced
3 spring onions (scallions), thinly sliced
2 garlic cloves, finely chopped
1 Tbsp Chinese rice wine
½ Tbsp sesame oil
½ Tbsp Mushroom Stir-Fry Sauce (page 155 or use shop-bought)
2 tsp dark soy sauce

For the marinated mushrooms
35g (2 cups) dried Chinese mushrooms
½ tsp cornflour (cornstarch)
1 tsp vegetable oil
1 tsp oyster sauce
½ tsp Chinese rice wine
1 tsp dark soy sauce
¼ tsp sugar
¼ tsp ground white pepper
½ tsp salt

Place the sticky rice in a large bowl and cover completely with water. Let stand for at least 2 hours or overnight.

Rinse the dried mushrooms under warm water and put into a large bowl. Cover with boiling water and soak for 15 minutes until soft, then gently squeeze the excess water out of the mushrooms. Remove and discard the stalks and cut the mushrooms into 6 slices. Mix the sliced mushrooms with the remaining marinade ingredients until thoroughly combined and let stand in the fridge for at least 2 hours.

Cut each lotus leaf in half down the middle. Place the leaves in a large bowl or container and cover with water, weighing the leaves down with a plate if necessary to keep them submerged. Leave to soak for 1 hour.

Drain the sticky rice well and transfer to a large bowl.

Heat 2 teaspoons of the oil in a wok over a high heat until shimmering. Add the shallot, spring onions and garlic and cook for about 2 minutes until softened. Add the mixture into the bowl of soaked sticky rice along with the Chinese rice wine, sesame oil, Mushroom Stir-Fry Sauce and dark soy sauce and combine well. In the same wok, heat the remaining teaspoon of oil over a high heat until shimmering. Add the marinated mushrooms and stir-fry for 2 minutes. Transfer to a plate.

Drain the lotus leaves, pat them dry with kitchen paper and spread out on a work surface. Place 2–3 tablespoons of sticky rice mixture into the centre of each lotus leaf, then add 1–2 tablespoons of mushroom mixture followed by another 2–3 tablespoons of sticky rice mixture.

Wrap each parcel by folding the end closest to you over the rice and then folding the left and right edges over the top, then rolling the rest of the leaf to form a tight package. Using kitchen string, tie up each package, making sure that all the leaves are securely wrapped.

Place the rice parcels into a steamer for 1½ hours; keep an eye on the water level, topping up with more boiling water if needed to prevent the steamer from boiling dry.

RICE PORRIDGE CONGEE

Congee is a very traditional Chinese dish and it dates back thousands of years. In ancient times, people named congee *chan*, 'the watery one'. In our house, congee was called soggy rice; Mum made it often and we ate bowls and bowls with lashings of light soy sauce. If we were lucky Mum would also make Chinese bread, which we would tear chunks off and dip into our bowls. The Chinese often eat congee for breakfast and on my last visit to Hong Kong, Dad and I would make the 15-minute pilgrimage from our hotel to go and sit in a rundown congee restaurant located in Kowloon.

15 MINUTES   **1½ HOURS**   **SERVES 2-3**

6 medium dried Chinese mushrooms
2 Tbsp Chinese pickled turnip, shredded (optional)
180g (1 cup) long-grain rice
3.5 litres (14 cups) water or vegetable stock
thumb-sized piece of fresh ginger, thinly sliced

Toppings (optional)
soy sauce
salted peanuts, crushed
spring onions (scallions), thinly sliced
crispy deep-fried onion, sliced
sesame seeds
crispy fried tofu pieces
salt to taste

Rinse the mushrooms under warm water and put into a large bowl of freshly boiled water. Soak for 15 minutes until soft, then gently squeeze the excess water out of the mushrooms. Remove and discard the stalks and cut the mushrooms into thin slices. If you are using pickled turnip rinse it under cold water to remove some of the salt and cut into bite-sized pieces.

Wash the rice thoroughly and drain well. Put into a large saucepan, add the water or stock, ginger and pickled turnip (if using) and bring to the boil. Once boiling, turn down to a simmer, add the mushrooms and cook for about 1½ hours. If it looks like the rice is becoming too thick, you can add more water; the congee wants to be of pouring consistency similar to wallpaper paste.

Serve with Chinese Breadsticks (page 136), a splash of soy sauce and sprinkled with a selection of your favourite toppings and season to taste.

SEASONED GLUTINOUS RICE

Though misleading in name, this rice dish doesn't actually contain any gluten at all and refers only to its texture; in Hong Kong and China it is referred to as sticky rice and made with grains that are very short and almost round. Seasoned or steamed, little can compare to the flavour; it's aromatic yet a little pungent and really does taste outstanding.

2 HRS 5 MINS   **30 MINUTES**   **SERVES 4**

450g (2½ cups) glutinous rice
2 Tbsp light soy sauce
⅛ tsp white pepper
½ tsp Chinese five spice
250ml (1 cup) water
½ Tbsp oil (vegetable, groundnut or coconut)
½ Tbsp sesame oil

Place the rice in a large bowl and wash under cold water, then rinse. Repeat this at least three times to remove some of the starch. Cover with cold water and allow to soak for 2 hours.

Drain the soaked rice, then add all of the remaining ingredients and mix well. Transfer the rice to a heatproof bowl, place into a steamer and steam for 30 minutes.

Serve piping hot.

CHINESE BAKED RICE

This dish is very popular in Hong Kong cafés; a bed of fried rice is topped with crispy-coated marinated mushrooms, then smothered in a rich aromatic tomato sauce and finally layered with oozing melted mozzarella. Asian-Italian fusion at its simplest.

35 MINUTES   **40 MINUTES**   **SERVES 4**

For the fried rice
1½ Tbsp oil (vegetable, groundnut or coconut)
250g (9oz) cooked steamed rice, cold (page 98 or use pre-cooked packets of rice)
1 Tbsp light soy sauce
½ Tbsp dark soy sauce
2 Tbsp Mushroom Stir-Fry Sauce (page 155 or use shop-bought)
½ tsp salt
1 tsp sesame oil

For the topping
1 Tbsp rice wine
2 Tbsp light soy sauce
½ tsp salt
½ tsp sugar
¼ tsp white pepper
3 large portobello mushrooms
4 Tbsp plain (all-purpose) flour
4 Tbsp oil (vegetable, groundnut or coconut)
2 garlic cloves, finely chopped
1 onion, sliced
1 x 400g (14oz) can chopped tomatoes
4 Tbsp tomato ketchup
65g (½ cup) grated mozzarella (omit if vegan)

First make the fried rice. Heat the oil in a wok over a medium-high heat, add the rice and cook for 2–3 minutes (remember this is fried rice so your wok needs to be hot enough that you can hear the ingredients sizzling as you cook). Add the light and dark soy sauces, Mushroom Stir-Fry sauce and salt and continue frying until the rice is completely heated through and piping hot. Remove from the heat, stir in the sesame oil and set to one side to cool.

Combine the rice wine, soy sauce, salt, sugar and white pepper in a large bowl and mix well. Marinate the mushrooms in the mixture for 30 minutes.

In a large bowl, coat the marinated mushrooms thoroughly in the flour. Heat a large non-stick frying pan over a medium-high heat, add 3 tablespoons of the oil and fry the mushrooms on both sides for 3–4 minutes until crispy and golden brown. Remove from the pan and drain on kitchen paper.

Preheat the oven to 200°C (400°F).

Place the wok back over a medium-high heat and add the remaining oil, garlic and onion and fry for 3–4 minutes, or until caramelised. Add the canned tomatoes and ketchup, bring to the boil and then turn down to a simmer, covering loosely and cooking for 5–10 minutes, or until the sauce has reduced by half.

In a baking tray or ovenproof dish, spread out the fried rice evenly and place the fried mushrooms on top. Pour over the sauce, ensuring all of the mushrooms and rice are covered. Lastly sprinkle with mozzarella (if using) and bake in the oven for 15 minutes, or until piping hot and bubbling. Serve immediately.

NOODLES

HONG KONG CRISPY NOODLES WITH MIXED VEGETABLES

I order this dish every time we eat at a Chinese restaurant; the crispy noodles soften under the rich aromatic gravy flecked with garlic. The vegetables are crunchy, as they have been cooked quickly to retain their bright vibrant colours. The combination of textures from crispy noodles to crunchy vegetables is simply sensational.

10 MINUTES   **10 MINUTES**   **SERVES 2**

1 nest of dried fine egg noodles (vegan option: use dried rice noodles/vermicelli)

1 Tbsp oil (vegetable, groundnut or coconut), plus extra for shallow frying

2 slices of fresh ginger

1 garlic clove, finely chopped

1 onion, sliced

1 carrot, sliced

30g (¼ cup) canned bamboo shoots, drained and sliced

3 baby corn cobs, halved lengthways

25g (¼ cup) mangetout (snow peas)

35g (¼ cup) canned straw mushrooms, drained and halved

handful of beansprouts

2 spring onions (scallions), halved and then sliced lengthways

1 Tbsp dark soy sauce

1 Tbsp light soy sauce

½ tsp white pepper

½ tsp salt

½ tsp sugar

2 Tbsp Mushroom Stir-Fry Sauce (page 155 or use shop-bought)

75ml (⅓ cup) vegetable stock

1 Tbsp cornflour (cornstarch) mixed with 2 Tbsp water

2 tsp sesame oil

Put the egg noodles into a bowl, cover with boiling water and leave for 2 minutes, or until soft, then drain and allow to cool.

Pour 250ml (1 cup) oil for shallow frying in a wok and place over a medium-high heat; once the oil begins to shimmer, carefully lower the drained noodles into the oil so they cover the entire bottom of the wok. Once golden brown and crispy, flip them over to brown the other side. Transfer to a wire rack or kitchen paper to drain.

Heat the tablespoon of oil in a wok and add the ginger and garlic, frying until fragrant. Add the onion and cook until translucent, followed by the carrot, bamboo shoots, baby corn, mangetout and straw mushrooms. Fry for 1 minute, then add the beansprouts and spring onions and mix well. Add the dark and light soy sauces, white pepper, salt, sugar, Mushroom Stir-Fry Sauce and vegetable stock and bring to the boil. Slowly pour in the cornflour mixture, stirring constantly until the sauce reaches the desired consistency. Remove from the heat and stir in the sesame oil.

Place the crispy noodles on to a large plate and using a pair of scissors, cut the noodle nest into quarters. Pour the vegetables over the noodles and serve.

VEGETABLE CHOW MEIN

As one of the top five most ordered dishes in the UK, chow mein (fried noodles) is truly loved. Take your time when cooking this dish; it needs a little TLC to make it all it can be. You want to scorch some of the noodles so they become crispy and caramelised, while the vegetables should be crunchy. Follow this simple recipe and you'll be a chow mein master in no time.

10 MINUTES   **10 MINUTES**   **SERVES 2**

2 nests of dried egg noodles (vegan alternative: use udon noodles)
1½ Tbsp oil (vegetable, groundnut or coconut)
1 small white onion, thinly sliced
½ red (bell) pepper, thinly sliced
3 baby corn cobs, halved lengthways
1 carrot, cut into strips
handful of beansprouts
30g (¼ cup) canned bamboo shoots, drained and sliced
½ tsp white pepper
½ tsp salt
½ tsp sugar
2 spring onions (scallions), halved and sliced lengthways
1 Tbsp Mushroom Stir-Fry Sauce (page 155 or use shop-bought)
1 Tbsp dark soy sauce
1 Tbsp light soy sauce
1 tsp sesame oil

If you are using dried egg noodles, put them into a bowl, cover with boiling water and leave for 3 minutes, or until soft, then drain and allow to cool.

Heat the oil in a non-stick wok and fry the onion, red pepper, baby corn and carrot for 2 minutes until soft. Add the beansprouts, bamboo shoots, white pepper, salt and sugar and stir for a further minute or two. Add the drained noodles and half of the spring onions and mix thoroughly, turning the heat to high. Fry for 2 minutes, ensuring you keep the ingredients moving.

Add the Mushroom Stir-Fry Sauce, dark and light soy sauces and mix well. Remove from the heat, add a drizzle of sesame oil, garnish with the remaining spring onions and serve.

HONG KONG-STYLE NOODLE SOUP WITH TOFU & CHINESE VEGETABLES

The cooked egg noodles should still be springy and chewy so don't be scared to slightly undercook them; once you add them to the hot soup they'll continue to cook a little longer. I like to eat my noodles with a dash of chilli sauce or chilli oil to amp up the flavour. This is a very traditional and widely eaten dish across China, Hong Kong and the world.

5 MINUTES　　**10 MINUTES**　　**SERVES 2**

1 litre (4 cups) vegetable stock
¼ tsp white pepper
thumb-sized piece of fresh ginger, sliced
½ Tbsp light soy sauce
1 nest of fresh egg noodles (vegan option: use dried rice noodles/ vermicelli)
200g (7oz) firm tofu, cut into bite-sized pieces
2 handfuls of your chosen Chinese vegetable (choy sum, bok choy, gai lan or Chinese Napa cabbage), cut into bite-sized pieces
1 tsp sesame oil
1 spring onion (scallion), thinly sliced
salt to taste

Put the stock, white pepper, sliced ginger and soy sauce into a saucepan, place over a medium heat and bring to a gentle simmer. Taste for seasoning.

Bring another saucepan of water to the boil, add the noodles and cook for 1 minute until tender but still springy (cook rice noodles for a little longer). Drain and place into 2 serving bowls.

Add the tofu and vegetables to your soup and return to the boil. Once boiling, remove the soup from the heat and gently pour over the noodles. Add a splash of sesame oil, a sprinkle of sliced spring onions and eat it while it's hot.

MUSHROOM LO MEIN

Unlike chow mein, in which noodles are fried to crispiness; lo mein is cooked in a sauce to keep them soft. You'll be surprised how much flavour they take on, providing you with a great comforting bowl of savoury, noodle-y delight.

10 MINUTES   **6 MINUTES**   **SERVES 2–3**

1 Tbsp rice wine
3 Tbsp Mushroom Stir-Fry Sauce (page 155 or use shop-bought)
2 Tbsp light soy sauce
2 tsp sugar
1 tsp Chinese five spice
1 Tbsp rice vinegar
¼ tsp white pepper
2 nests of fresh lo mein egg noodles (vegan option: use fresh udon noodles)
2 Tbsp oil (vegetable, groundnut or coconut)
1 garlic clove, finely chopped
2 spring onions (scallions), cut in half and then into thin strips
1 carrot, cut into matchsticks
1 large portobello mushroom, cut into bite-sized pieces
6–8 baby corn cobs, quartered lengthways
30g (¼ cup) canned water chestnuts, drained and sliced
½ Tbsp sesame oil

Combine the rice wine, Mushroom Stir-Fry Sauce, soy sauce, sugar, Chinese five spice, rice vinegar and white pepper in a bowl. Set to one side.

Loosen the noodles by soaking in a bowl of warm water, drain and set to one side.

Place a wok over a medium-high heat and add the oil, garlic and spring onions and fry for around 20 seconds until fragrant. Add the carrot and mushrooms and fry for a further 2 minutes, then add the baby corn, water chestnuts and the loosened noodles. Fry for a further 2 minutes, add the sauce mixture and continue to fry until all of the ingredients are combined well and warmed through. Remove from the heat, stir in the sesame oil and transfer to serving bowls.

VEGETABLE UDON IN YELLOW BEAN SAUCE WITH CASHEW NUTS

These soft noodles are drenched in a richly subtle barbecue-style sauce that clings to every strand. The vegetables still have their snap and when eaten alongside creamy cashew nuts it really is a perfect mouthful.

5 MINUTES   **5 MINUTES**   **SERVES 2-3**

1 Tbsp rice wine
4 Tbsp yellow bean sauce
1 Tbsp light soy sauce
4 Tbsp vegetable stock
2 tsp sugar
2 nests of fresh udon noodles
2 Tbsp oil (vegetable, groundnut
   or coconut)
½ onion, sliced
1 carrot, cut into matchsticks
70g (½ cup) canned straw
   mushrooms, drained and halved
60g (½ cup) bamboo shoots, drained
6–8 baby corn cobs, quartered
   lengthways
½ Tbsp sesame oil
½ cup cashew nuts, roughly
   crumbled

Combine the rice wine, yellow bean sauce, soy sauce, stock and sugar in a bowl. Set to one side.

Loosen the noodles by soaking in a bowl of warm water, then drain and set to one side.

Place a wok over a medium-high heat and add the oil, onion, carrot, straw mushrooms, bamboo shoots and baby corn and fry for 3 minutes. Next add the loosened udon noodles and continue to fry for a further minute.

Add the sauce mixture and continue to fry until all of the ingredients are well acquainted and warmed through. Remove from the heat, stir in the sesame oil and transfer to serving bowls. Lastly, sprinkle with crumbled cashew nuts and enjoy.

UDON NOODLES WITH FIVE SPICE TOFU

Soft noodles sitting in a rich broth, surrounded by vibrant vegetables, unctuous five spice-marinated tofu and sprinkled with sesame seeds for texture and a nutty flavour – what's not to love?

5 MINUTES   **10 MINUTES**   **SERVES 2**

2 Tbsp oil (vegetable, groundnut or coconut)
1 Tbsp grated fresh ginger
2 garlic cloves, finely chopped
2 Tbsp miso paste
1 litre (4 cups) vegetable stock
¼ tsp salt
pinch of white pepper
280g (9oz) firm tofu, cut into bite-sized pieces
2 Tbsp light soy sauce
½ tsp Chinese five spice
1 tsp sesame oil
2 nests (170g/6oz) fresh udon noodles
1 cup shredded Napa cabbage
50g (1 cup) beansprouts
2 Tbsp black and white sesame seeds, toasted
2 spring onions (scallions), thinly sliced

Heat 1 tablespoon of the oil in a saucepan over a medium heat and fry the ginger and garlic until fragrant. Add the miso paste and mix well, followed by the vegetable stock, salt and pepper. Bring to the boil and, once boiling, turn down immediately to a simmer.

Heat the remaining tablespoon of oil in a non-stick frying pan, add the tofu and fry on all sides until lightly browned, then add the soy sauce and Chinese five spice, mixing well to coat each piece of tofu thoroughly. Finally add the sesame oil and mix well.

Bring a large saucepan of water to the boil and add the fresh noodles; cook for about 90 seconds. Drain and place into serving bowls. In the same boiling water, blanch the cabbage for 30 seconds, drain and neatly place on to one-third of your bowl of noodles. Repeat for the beansprouts. Ladle the soup over the vegetables and noodles, then place your cooked tofu on to the final third of your bowl. Sprinkle the entire dish with the sesame seeds and spring onions to serve.

UDON NOODLE CURRY SOUP

We all love a good curry and this dish combines the authentic Chinese curry taste with a soup. Served on top of soft noodles, crunchy beansprouts and meaty mushrooms, it's sure to satisfy those curry cravings.

10 MINUTES   **20 MINUTES**   **SERVES 2**

2 Tbsp oil (vegetable, groundnut or coconut)
1 medium white onion, sliced
1 medium carrot, cut into matchsticks
50g (½ cup) beansprouts
½ large portobello mushroom, cut into thin strips
750ml (3 cups) vegetable stock
250ml (1 cup) curry sauce (see below)
1 Tbsp light soy sauce
¼ tsp salt (or to taste)
2 nests (170g/6oz) fresh udon noodles
2 spring onions (scallions), thinly sliced

For the curry sauce
1 Tbsp oil (vegetable, groundnut or coconut)
2 onions, finely diced
5 garlic cloves, finely chopped
2 carrots, finely diced
1 celery stick, finely diced
2 Tbsp plain (all-purpose) flour
1½ Tbsp curry powder (use your favourite: mild, medium or hot)
600ml (2½ cups) vegetable stock
½ Tbsp honey
1½ Tbsp soy sauce
1 bay leaf
1 tsp garam masala

For the curry sauce, heat the oil in a saucepan, then add the onions and garlic and cook until softened. Stir in the carrots and celery and cook over a low heat for 10–12 minutes. Add the flour and curry powder and cook for 1 minute. Gradually pour in the stock, stirring constantly until combined, then add the honey, soy sauce and bay leaf. Slowly bring to the boil. Simmer for 15 minutes, or until the sauce thickens but is still of pouring consistency. If your sauce is too thick, add a splash of water to loosen it. Stir in the garam masala, then strain the curry sauce through a sieve and set to one side.

Heat the oil in a saucepan over a medium-high heat, add the onion and carrot and fry until lightly browned. Add the beansprouts and mushrooms and fry for a further minute.

Add the stock, curry sauce and soy sauce and mix well until smoothly combined. Bring to the boil then turn down the heat to a low simmer. Taste for seasoning and add salt if needed.

Bring a large saucepan of water to the boil, add the fresh noodles and cook for about 90 seconds. Drain and place into serving bowls. Pour over your curry soup, garnish with spring onions and serve.

CHILLI TOFU RAMEN

For those of you who have a sweet tooth but enjoy a hint of heat, this dish is definitely one for you. Soft curly noodles, sitting in a fiery, aromatic broth, topped with crispy, chewy tofu and lavishly smothered in a sweet chilli sauce.

 10 MINUTES   **10 MINUTES**   **SERVES 2**

½ tsp oil (vegetable, groundnut or coconut)

2 garlic cloves, crushed

2 slices of fresh ginger

750ml (3 cups) vegetable stock

3 Tbsp soy sauce

¼ tsp chilli powder

2 nests of dried ramen noodles

2 Tbsp toasted sesame seeds

2 spring onions (scallions), finely chopped

For the tofu

280g (9oz) firm tofu, cut into bite-sized pieces

2 Tbsp cornflour (cornstarch)

1½ Tbsp oil

2 garlic cloves, finely chopped

6 Tbsp sweet chilli sauce (shop-bought or page 154)

To prepare the tofu, dry the cubes on kitchen paper, then put into a bowl and coat with the cornflour. Heat a non-stick frying pan over a medium-high heat, add the oil and fry until golden brown. Add the garlic and fry for 30 seconds until fragrant, then stir in the sweet chilli sauce. Once all the ingredients are combined, remove from the heat.

Heat the oil in a large saucepan over a medium-high heat, add the garlic and ginger and fry for 30 seconds. Add the stock, soy sauce and chilli powder. Bring to the boil, then turn down to a simmer while you cook the noodles.

Cook the ramen noodles in a saucepan of boiling water for 3 minutes until tender; drain and transfer to serving bowls. Pour the soup over your noodles, arrange the chilli tofu pieces on top and finally sprinkle with the sesame seeds and spring onions.

SINGAPORE RICE NOODLES

This dish was actually invented in Hong Kong and is commonly found in Cantonese restaurants all across the world, but most oddly, not in Singapore. Seasoned with curry powder and cooked with a selection of mixed vegetables, these delicious firm rice noodles are equally smoky and spicy.

10 MINUTES   **10 MINUTES**   **SERVES 2**

2 nests of dried rice noodles (vermicelli)
2 Tbsp vegetable oil
1 Tbsp grated fresh ginger
1 red chilli, de-seeded and finely chopped
1 red (bell) pepper, de-seeded and sliced
1 small carrot, cut into matchsticks
handful of beansprouts
1½ Tbsp medium curry powder
1 tsp crushed dried chillies
¼ tsp white pepper
1 Tbsp light soy sauce
1 Tbsp dark soy sauce
1 tsp sugar
1 Tbsp rice vinegar
1 egg, beaten (omit if vegan)
dash of sesame oil
2 spring onions (scallions), cut in half and thinly sliced lengthways

Cook the rice noodles in a saucepan of boiling water for about 2 minutes until tender, then drain and set aside.

Heat the oil in a wok and stir-fry the ginger and fresh chilli for a few seconds. Add the red pepper, carrot and beansprouts and cook for another minute before adding the curry powder and combining well.

Add the noodles to the wok, mixing the ingredients thoroughly and stir-fry for 2 minutes. Season with the dried chillies, white pepper, light and dark soy sauces, sugar and rice vinegar and continue to fry for another minute, stirring until all of the flavours are combined. Create a well in the centre of your wok by pushing the noodles up the sides, then add the beaten egg, stirring gently until the egg is cooked through. Combine with the rest of the ingredients.

Remove from the heat and stir in the sesame oil. Transfer to serving bowls, sprinkle over the spring onions and serve immediately.

DAN DAN NOODLES

The name refers to a type of carrying pole (*dan dan*) that was used by walking street hawkers who sold the dish to passers-by. Also known as 'peddlers noodles', the dish originates from Chinese Sichuan cuisine. A quick and tasty dish of noodles served in a spicy sauce containing vegetables, chilli oil, Sichuan pepper and spring onions.

10 MINUTES   **15 MINUTES**   **SERVES 2–3**

340g (12oz) udon noodles (or you can use your favourite type of noodle)

3 Tbsp vegetable oil

200g (7oz) mix of bamboo shoots, water chestnuts, carrot, onion and mushrooms, finely diced

2 Tbsp grated fresh ginger

½ tsp Chinese five spice

200ml (¾ cup) vegetable stock

2 Tbsp chilli oil, (or to taste; optional)

2 Tbsp rice vinegar

2 Tbsp Chinese rice wine

2 Tbsp light soy sauce

4 tsp tahini

1 tsp Sichuan peppercorns, coarsely ground

½ tsp sugar

4 Tbsp chopped roasted peanuts

4 spring onions (scallions), thinly sliced

salt and freshly ground black pepper

Bring a large saucepan of water to the boil and add the noodles. Cook until tender – for about 1 minute for fresh noodles and 2–3 minutes for dried noodles – but still slightly firm to the bite, then drain and transfer to a bowl of iced water to quickly chill. Drain well.

Heat the oil in a large wok over a medium-high heat until smoking. Add the diced vegetables and a pinch of salt and pepper and cook until tender. Add the ginger and Chinese five spice and continue cooking until the ginger is fragrant.

Stir in the vegetable stock, chilli oil, rice vinegar, Chinese rice wine, soy sauce, tahini, Sichuan peppercorns and sugar and bring to the boil, then reduce the heat and simmer gently until the sauce thickens – this can take up to 7–10 minutes.

Add the drained noodles to the wok and toss well in the sauce. Once the noodles are heated through, check and adjust the seasoning to your taste. Transfer to serving bowls and top with the peanuts and spring onions. Serve immediately.

TOFU, PICKLED CABBAGE & BLACK BEANS ON RICE NOODLES

This is traditional Cantonese cooking at its very best. It combines a rich garlic and black bean sauce with pickled cabbage and crispy tofu, sitting on top of firm rice noodles in an aromatic ginger-spiced soup, seasoned with nutty sesame oil.

10 MINUTES   **15 MINUTES**   **SERVES 2**

2 nests of dried rice noodles
  (vermicelli)
2 Tbsp oil (vegetable, groundnut
  or coconut)
200g (7oz) firm tofu, cut into small
  bite-sized pieces
thumb-sized piece of fresh ginger,
  peeled and sliced
4 garlic cloves, roughly chopped
3 Tbsp fermented black beans
1 small can Chinese pickled
  vegetables, drained
1 Tbsp dark soy sauce
1 Tbsp light soy sauce
125ml (½ cup) vegetable stock
1 Tbsp cornflour (cornstarch) mixed
  with 2 Tbsp water
1 tsp sesame oil

For the soup
3cm (1¼in) piece of fresh ginger,
  sliced
1 Tbsp soy sauce
800ml (3¼ cups) vegetable stock
½ tsp white pepper
1 tsp salt

Soak the rice noodles in a large bowl of boiling water for 10 minutes, then drain and set to one side

Heat 1 tablespoon of the oil in a wok and fry the tofu pieces over a medium heat until golden brown on all sides, then drain on kitchen paper and set to one side.

For the soup, put the ginger, soy sauce, vegetable stock, white pepper and salt into a large saucepan and bring to the boil, then turn down to a simmer.

Place your wok over a medium-high heat, add the remaining tablespoon of oil along with the ginger and garlic and fry for 30 seconds until fragrant. Add the black beans and fried tofu and fry for a minute before adding the pickled vegetables, dark and light soy sauces and vegetable stock. Bring to the boil, then turn down the heat and simmer for 3 minutes. Increase the heat to high and slowly add the cornflour mixture, stirring constantly to thicken the sauce. Remove from the heat.

Place the cooked rice noodles into serving bowls and pour over the soup so that the noodles are completely covered. Spoon over the tofu and black bean topping and finally drizzle with the sesame oil.

HOT & SOUR CHINESE VEGETABLES WITH MUNG BEAN NOODLES

These crispy strips of tofu, with crunchy vegetables in a tangy, sweet and subtly pungent chilli sauce are sure to get your taste buds tingling. All served over soft mung bean noodles and topped with nutty toasted sesame seeds, this dish will have your guests calling for a second helping.

 10 MINUTES   **10 MINUTES**   **SERVES 2**

2 nests of glass (mung bean) noodles
1 Tbsp sesame seeds
2 Tbsp groundnut oil
100g (3½oz) firm tofu, cut into 1 x 5cm (½ x 2in) strips
1 onion, sliced
1 carrot, sliced
30g (¼ cup) canned bamboo shoots, drained and sliced
30g (¼ cup) canned water chestnuts, drained and sliced
½ red (bell) pepper, sliced
2 spring onions (scallions), thinly sliced

For the hot & sour sauce
2 Tbsp rice wine
1½ Tbsp dark soy sauce
2 Tbsp rice vinegar
150ml (⅔ cup) vegetable stock
1 Tbsp tomato purée (paste)
2 tsp chilli bean sauce
½ tsp white pepper
2 tsp sugar

Place the glass noodles into a large bowl, cover with boiling water and leave to soak for 3–5 minutes. Once the noodles are soft, drain and set to one side.

Place a dry wok over a medium-low heat (make sure it is completely dry by wiping with kitchen paper before you start). Add the sesame seeds and slowly toast for 2–3 minutes, or until they have turned golden brown and fragrant. Transfer to a plate and allow to cool.

Heat 1 tablespoon of the oil in the wok over a medium heat and fry the tofu strips for 2–3 minutes on each side until they are golden brown. They should be crispy on the outside but soft inside. Transfer to kitchen paper to drain.

Add the hot and sour sauce ingredients to a saucepan. Bring the sauce to the boil and then lower the heat and simmer to reduce the sauce by a third, then remove from the heat and set aside.

Heat the remaining tablespoon of oil in the wok over a medium heat and add the onion, carrot, bamboo shoots, water chestnuts and red pepper, stir-frying until tender, about 2–3 minutes. Add the tofu pieces along with the hot and sour sauce and combine well. Arrange the noodles in a bowl or plate and pour over the tofu and vegetables. Sprinkle with the spring onions and the toasted sesame seeds. Serve and enjoy.

STIR-FRIED HO FUN

Noodles are an essential ingredient and a staple of the Chinese diet; widely produced across Hong Kong and China, they come in many forms. Ho fun is a type of noodle made with rice flour and is often served with vegetables in Cantonese restaurants. The noodles in this recipe are fried alongside a mix of crunchy and soft vegetables in a traditional Cantonese-style sauce.

10 MINUTES　　**10 MINUTES**　　**SERVES 2**

1 packet fresh ho fun (rice stick) noodles (360–450g/12–14oz depending on the brand available)
1 Tbsp oil (vegetable, groundnut or coconut)
3 slices of fresh ginger
2 garlic cloves, finely chopped
1 onion, sliced
1 carrot, sliced
5 baby corn cobs, halved lengthways
30g (¼ cup) bamboo shoots, drained
35g (¼ cup) canned straw mushrooms, drained
3 Tbsp Mushroom Stir-Fry Sauce (page 155 or use shop-bought)
1 Tbsp light soy sauce
pinch of white pepper
1 tsp sugar
4 Tbsp vegetable stock
1 bok choy, quartered
1 tsp sesame oil
salt to taste

Place the ho fun noodles in a large bowl of warm water and carefully separate the noodles, then drain and set to one side.

Heat the oil in a wok over a medium-high heat. Add the ginger and garlic and after 30 seconds, add the onion and fry until translucent. Add the carrot, baby corn, bamboo shoots and straw mushrooms and fry for a further 2–3 minutes.

Add the drained noodles to the wok and mix well. After 2 minutes of cooking, add the Mushroom Stir-Fry Sauce, soy sauce, pepper, sugar, vegetable stock and bok choy. Stir gently to combine and heat thoroughly; check the seasoning and add salt if required. Remove from the heat, drizzle with the sesame oil and stir through before serving.

MUSHROOM TERIYAKI WITH SOBA NOODLES

This dish is a perfect combination of meaty portobello mushrooms pan-seared with sweet chilli sauce. With its crispy crust, springy soba noodles, and sweet honey and sour vinegar teriyaki sauce, it is utterly irresistible.

5 MINUTES   **15 MINUTES**   **SERVES 2**

120g (4½oz) soba noodles
1 Tbsp oil (vegetable, groundnut or coconut)
2 large portobello mushrooms, de-stalked and cleaned
2 Tbsp Sweet Chilli Sauce (page 154 or use shop-bought)
3 Tbsp honey (vegan option: use agave or maple syrup)
3 Tbsp rice vinegar
1½ Tbsp light soy sauce
handful of long-stem broccoli
1 red chilli, finely diced
1 Tbsp sesame seeds, toasted
salt to taste

Put the noodles into a deep saucepan, pour over boiling water and allow to gently simmer for about 5–6 minutes while you are cooking the mushrooms.

Heat the oil in a large wok, add the portobello mushrooms and cook over a medium-high heat for 4–5 minutes on one side until browned, then turn, sprinkle with salt and the Sweet Chilli Sauce and cook for a further 4–5 minutes until browned on the other side. Remove from the pan and set to one side.

Add 125ml (½ cup) of the soba noodle cooking water to the same wok with the honey, vinegar and soy sauce. Now add the broccoli along with half the chopped chilli. Cook over a medium-high heat for 6 minutes; if the sauce starts to dry, add a little more water.

Once the broccoli is tender, drain the noodles and add them to the wok, stirring through to ensure the noodles are well coated with the sauce. Sprinkle over the remaining chilli and transfer to serving plates. Slice the cooked mushrooms and arrange over the top of the noodles. Sprinkle with the toasted sesame seeds and enjoy.

SIDES

ASIAN SLAW

This salad, filled with its crunchy cabbage, sweet carrots and savoury spring onions, delivers on all of the five flavours of Chinese cuisine. It's salty, spicy, sour, sweet and bitter – a party in your mouth!

15 MINUTES   **SERVES 2-4**

¼ white cabbage, shredded
¼ red cabbage, shredded
2 carrots, grated
thumb-sized piece of fresh ginger, peeled and grated
2 spring onions (scallions), halved and shredded lengthways
1 Thai red chilli, finely chopped
zest and juice of 2 limes
2 Tbsp toasted sesame seeds
2 Tbsp sunflower oil
1½ Tbsp muscovado sugar
2 tsp salt (or to taste)

In a large bowl, combine the cabbages, carrots, ginger, spring onions, chilli and lime zest and lemon juice, followed by the sesame seeds, sunflower oil and sugar. Season to taste.

Tip
After you have removed the zest from the limes, place each lime in the microwave for 10 seconds on full power to make them easier to juice.

CHINESE BREADSTICKS

These deep-fried Chinese breadsticks (*youtiao*) are golden and chewy. No one can make Chinese bread quite like momma Wan. It was always a treat when my mum found the time to cook up a batch along with a huge pot of steaming congee.

4½ HOURS   **20 MINUTES**   **SERVES 2-4**

250g (2 cups) plain (all-purpose) flour
1 egg (vegan option: 1 Tbsp vegetable oil mixed with ½ tsp baking powder)
½ tsp salt
1½ tsp baking powder
1 Tbsp milk (vegan option: soya milk)
2 Tbsp softened butter (vegan option: vegetable or olive oil spread)
75ml (⅓ cup) water
1 litre (4 cups) oil (vegetable, groundnut or coconut) for frying

Using a stand mixer fitted with the dough hook attachment, mix the flour, egg, salt, baking powder, milk and softened butter together on the lowest setting. Keeping the speed at 'stir', slowly add the water in two or three batches. Increase the speed to medium and knead the dough for 10 minutes. The dough should feel very soft, but should not stick to the bowl. Cover the dough with a damp cloth or cling film (plastic wrap) and let rest for 10 minutes.

On a clean, lightly floured surface, form the dough into a long flat loaf shape, about 1cm (½in) thick and 10cm (4in) wide. Take the time to make it truly uniform. Place it in the centre of a large piece of cling film on a baking sheet or long, flat plate and wrap the dough, tucking the two ends of the film under the loaf, ensuring that the dough is completely covered. Refrigerate overnight if possible but for at least 2 hours.

Take out the dough and let it sit on the work surface (wrapped) for 1–2 hours until the dough comes up to room temperature and is soft to the touch. This step is critical. If you don't let the dough come back to room temperature, it won't fry properly.

Now heat the oil for frying in your wok. You can also use a wide, deep-sided frying pan. The goal is to have a large vessel, so that you can produce authentically long breadsticks. Use a medium heat to slowly bring the oil up to 180°C (350°F).

While the oil is heating up, you can unwrap the dough. Gently flip the dough on to a lightly floured surface, peeling off the cling film. Lightly flour the top of the dough. Next, cut the dough into 2.5cm (1in) wide strips (try to cut an even number of strips), then stack the strips two by two and press down the centre, lengthways, with a chopstick, to make an impression. Hold the two ends of each piece, and gently stretch the dough to around 20cm (8in).

Once the oil is ready, carefully lower one of the stretched dough pieces into the oil. If the temperature is right, the dough should come to the surface right away. Quickly turn the dough in a continuous motion for about a minute. You can fry one or two dough pieces at a time – just be sure to take the time to continuously roll the dough in the oil. The breadsticks are done once they turn light golden brown. Try not to over-fry them as they become unpleasantly crunchy rather than chewy and delicious. Drain on kitchen paper while you fry the remaining dough strips.

Food Fact
Youtiao is eaten at breakfast and is served alongside congee or soya milk (pictured on page 104). Congee street food hawkers also serve the bread rolled inside a rice roll known as *cheong fun*.

EGGLESS OMELETTE

This wonderful eggless omelette recipe is perfect for breakfasts and light lunches. Just add your favourite veggies, vegan cheese or spice it up with garlic, onion & chilli powder and sautéed mushrooms.

5 MINUTES   **5 MINUTES**   **SERVES 2**

125g (1 cup) gram flour
1 tsp baking powder
40g (⅓ cup) plain (all-purpose) flour
1 tsp salt
250ml (1 cup) water
2 tbsp oil

Combine all of the dry ingredients together in a large bowl. Slowly whisk in enough water to make a batter the consistency of coconut milk, adding the water in small batches and mixing after each addition; this will take 2–3 minutes. Place a non-stick frying pan over a medium-high heat, add a tablespoon of oil and heat until you can see a little bit of smoke rising from the pan. Add a ladle of the batter and cook for 60–90 seconds, or until it's just starting to colour. Flip the omelette over and cook for another 30–60 seconds. Transfer to kitchen paper and allow to cool. Once cooled, cut the omelette into strips about 1cm (½in) thick.

ASPARAGUS WITH GINGER SOY

Juicy, crisp asparagus and mangetout are served in a rich umami soy sauce with the underlying heat of ginger.

---

5 MINUTES   **15 MINUTES**   **SERVES 2-4**

1 Tbsp vegetable oil
100g (¾ cup) raw cashew nuts
thumb-sized piece of fresh ginger,
   peeled and cut into
   thin matchsticks
1 garlic clove, finely chopped
2 bunches of asparagus
150g (5oz) mangetout (snow peas),
   trimmed
1 Tbsp soy sauce
1 Tbsp rice wine vinegar
1 Tbsp sesame oil

Heat half the oil in a wok over a medium heat. Once the wok is hot, add the cashew nuts and stir-fry for 1–2 minutes until toasted. Transfer to a plate lined with kitchen paper.

Pour the remaining oil into the wok and place over a medium-high heat. Add the ginger and garlic and stir-fry for 30 seconds until fragrant. Add the asparagus and mangetout and stir-fry for a further 2 minutes until tender. Pour in the soy sauce and rice wine vinegar and stir-fry for 1 minute, or until heated through. Remove from the heat, drizzle with the sesame oil and sprinkle with the cashew nuts. Serve and enjoy.

Tip
The best-tasting asparagus are always the ones that are super-fresh. Asparagus tips have the best flavour, so make sure they are firm and not wilting. The stalks should be plump and firm, and the tips should be tightly closed. When you buy your asparagus, store it standing upright in cold, fresh water.

CHINESE BROCCOLI IN GARLIC & GINGER SAUCE

Ginger has been medically proven to have many health benefits and is one of the Holy Trinity ingredients of Chinese cooking. Aromatic and so full of flavour, try this fast and simple recipe when you're just having 'one of those days' or if you simply need a boost; feel yourself being bathed in this naturally healing root.

5 MINUTES   **5 MINUTES**   **SERVES 2**

340g (12oz) gai lan (Chinese broccoli) or you can use long-stem broccoli
1 Tbsp vegetable oil
3 slices of fresh ginger
1 garlic clove, finely chopped
1 tsp sesame oil

For the sauce
75ml (⅓ cup) vegetable stock
1 Tbsp Chinese rice wine
2 tsp grated fresh ginger
½ tsp salt
½ tsp sugar
1 tsp cornflour (cornstarch)

First make the sauce. Combine the vegetable stock, Chinese rice wine, ginger, salt, sugar and cornflour in a bowl and set to one side.

Cut the broccoli into 5cm (2in) long pieces, keeping the stalk ends separate from the leaves.

Place a wok over a high heat. Once hot, add the oil, sliced ginger and garlic and stir-fry for 20 seconds, or until the ginger and garlic are fragrant. Add the broccoli stalks and stir-fry for 2 minutes, then add a splash of water to create some steam. Once the stalks are tender, add the broccoli leaves and stir-fry for 1 minute more. Add the sauce ingredients and continually stir until the sauce has thickened and is coating the vegetables. Transfer to a serving dish, add a dash of sesame oil and enjoy.

Health benefits of ginger
Ginger is among the healthiest (and most delicious) spices on the planet. It is loaded with nutrients and bioactive compounds that have powerful benefits for your body and brain. Ginger is used to treat many forms of nausea, including morning sickness and seasickness. It can reduce muscular pain, is a natural anti-inflammatory, can help lower blood sugars and treat indigestion.

BEANSPROUTS WITH GARLIC & ONION

The trick to making this dish taste like it was bought from a Chinese takeaway is the white pepper; the subtle background heat transforms the dish, giving it a further depth of flavour. Simple, wholesome and totally moreish.

5 MINUTES   **8 MINUTES**   **SERVES 2–3**

1 Tbsp oil (vegetable, groundnut or coconut)
2 garlic cloves, roughly chopped
3 spring onions (scallions), halved and then thinly sliced lengthways
1 large onion, sliced
500g (1lb 2oz) beansprouts
2 Tbsp Mushroom Stir-Fry Sauce (page 155 or use shop-bought)
¼ tsp white pepper
¼ tsp salt (or to taste)
1 tsp sugar
1 Tbsp light soy sauce
1 tsp dark soy sauce
125ml (½ cup) vegetable stock
1 Tbsp cornflour (cornstarch) mixed with 2 Tbsp water
1 tsp sesame oil

Pour the oil into a wok, place over a medium-high heat and fry the garlic and spring onions for 30 seconds, or until fragrant. Add the onion and cook for a further minute, then toss in the beansprouts and continue cooking for another minute.

Add the Mushroom Stir-Fry Sauce, pepper, salt, sugar, light and dark soy sauces and vegetable stock and heat thoroughly for 2–3 minutes.

Slowly add the cornflour mixture to the beansprouts, stirring continuously to thicken the sauce. Remove from the heat, stir in the sesame oil and serve.

SPICED BOK CHOY

Here tender bok choy is stir-fried in a fiery aromatic Cantonese sauce. Stir-frying is a quick cooking method that results in tender yet crisp vegetables that retain more of their important nutrients and lush colours.

10 MINUTES   **5 MINUTES**   **SERVES 2**

400g (14oz) baby bok choy
1 Tbsp oil (vegetable, groundnut or coconut)
1 Tbsp grated fresh ginger
1 garlic clove, finely chopped
1 small red bird's-eye chilli, finely chopped
1 Tbsp rice wine
1 tsp sugar
½ Tbsp Mushroom Stir-Fry Sauce (page 155 or use shop-bought)
1 Tbsp light soy sauce
½ tsp sesame oil

Trim the ends of the bok choy. Wash, pat dry with kitchen paper and set aside.

Heat a large non-stick wok over a medium-high heat. Add the oil, ginger and garlic and fry for 30 seconds until fragrant. Add the chilli and cook for a further 30 seconds. Next add the bok choy and rice wine and stir-fry for 1 minute before adding the sugar, Mushroom Stir-Fry Sauce and soy sauce. Cook for 1 minute, or until the bok choy is tender. Remove from the heat, drizzle with the sesame oil and serve warm.

CHILLI STIR-FRIED LETTUCE

The quick cooking of this dish shocks the lettuce into becoming even more vibrant and green. A very simple, yet ever so tasty recipe that will get you scratching your head as to why you haven't tried stir-frying iceberg lettuce before.

5 MINUTES   **5 MINUTES**   **SERVES 2-3**

1 large iceberg lettuce
2 Tbsp oil (vegetable, groundnut or coconut)
3 garlic cloves, very thinly sliced
1 green bird's-eye chilli, thinly sliced
3 Tbsp Mushroom Stir-Fry Sauce (page 155 or use shop-bought)
sesame oil, to serve

Remove the core from the lettuce, rinse and drain well. Halve the lettuce and cut the leaves into large bite-sized pieces, as they will wilt when cooked.

Heat the oil in a wok over a high heat and add the garlic and chilli, keeping them moving so they don't burn. After 20–30 seconds add the lettuce and the Mushroom Stir-Fry Sauce and cook until the leaves wilt, about 2 minutes. Turn off the heat, add a splash of sesame oil and serve immediately.

NAPA CABBAGE WITH MUSHROOM SAUCE

This is a great dish – simple to prepare and cook and has heaps of flavour. The rich mushroom sauce clings to the Napa leaves and every mouthful is juicy and salty, with that umami smoothness we all crave.

5 MINUTES   **5 MINUTES**   **SERVES 2–3**

2 Tbsp oil (vegetable, groundnut or coconut)
1 medium Napa cabbage, cored and sliced
1 medium portobello mushroom, thinly sliced
3 Tbsp Mushroom Stir-Fry Sauce (page 155 or use shop-bought)
1 Tbsp light soy sauce
1 tsp sesame oil

Heat the oil in a non-stick frying pan over a medium heat and, once hot, fry the cabbage for 2–3 minutes. Add the sliced mushroom and cook for a further minute, before stirring through the Mushroom Stir-Fry Sauce and soy sauce. Once completely combined, transfer to a serving plate, drizzle with the sesame oil and enjoy.

HONEY RICE WINE BROCCOLI STEMS

Get your wok super-hot as this dish only takes a few minutes to cook, leaving the broccoli stems crisp and succulent to eat. The fermented rice wine complements the sweet sticky honey, which helps the sauce cling to the broccoli stems.

5 MINUTES **5 MINUTES** **SERVES 2**

340g (12oz) long-stem broccoli
1 Tbsp oil (vegetable, groundnut or coconut)
2 Tbsp Chinese rice wine
1½ Tbsp honey (vegan option: use agave syrup, maple syrup, brown rice syrup or molasses)
¼ tsp salt (or to taste)

Trim the broccoli so that each piece is roughly the same length.

Place a non-stick wok over a medium-high heat and, once hot, add the oil. Add the broccoli and fry for 1 minute, then add a splash of water to create some steam and quickly toss the broccoli in the wok. Pour in the rice wine and honey and add salt to taste, then cook over a high heat for 1–2 minutes, or until the liquid has reduced by half. Serve hot.

SAUCES, DIPS & PICKLING

SOY PICKLED CUCUMBER

A great side dish to any meal, or just to snack on when you're a little peckish. The rich soy sauce delivers a smooth and silky eating experience, while the sweet vinegar makes these little cucumbers so totally moreish that each bite will have you going back for more.

5 MINUTES   **5 MINUTES**   **SERVES 3-4**   **2 HOURS**

500g (1lb 2oz) baby cucumbers
4 Tbsp light soy sauce
4 Tbsp water
50g (¼ cup) sugar
4 Tbsp rice vinegar
2 Tbsp Chinese black vinegar
2 thumb-sized pieces of fresh ginger

Cut the baby cucumbers into thin slices and put into a large glass bowl or jar.

Put the light soy sauce, water, sugar, rice vinegar, black vinegar and fresh ginger into a saucepan and place over a medium-low heat. Bring to a gentle boil and simmer until the sugar is completely dissolved. Remove from the heat.

Pour the vinegar liquid over the sliced cucumbers, ensuring they are fully submerged under the liquid. Cover and place in the fridge for 2 hours before eating. Eat within 1 week.

SWEET PICKLED GINGER

This is a great ingredient: with its subtle heat and complementary sweetness it can be eaten on its own, in a salad or as part of a dish. Traditionally prepared as a preserve, this ingredient is widely used in many Asian cuisines across the world.

5 MINUTES   **5 MINUTES**   **MAKES 1 SMALL JAR**   **3 DAYS**

340g (12oz) fresh ginger
250ml (1 cup) rice vinegar
50g (¼ cup) granulated sugar
1 tsp salt

Peel the ginger and cut into thin slices while you bring a saucepan of water to the boil. Blanch the sliced ginger for 20–30 seconds, remove from the water, drain and place into a sterilised jar.

Place a saucepan over a medium-low heat and add the rice vinegar, sugar and salt. Dissolve the sugar and salt gently and bring to the boil. Remove from the heat.

Carefully pour the hot vinegar mixture into the jar to completely cover the ginger. Seal and allow to cool completely. Leave to pickle in the fridge. The pickled ginger will be ready to eat after 3 days and can be stored in the fridge for up to 3 months.

CHINESE PICKLED VEGETABLES

This is a great side to rich or spicy dishes as it acts as a palate cleanser as you eat. It is especially good with Chinese-style curries or on top of a tofu burger – not only does it introduce a sour–sweet note, the vegetables are still crunchy, adding another texture dimension to each bite.

10 MINUTES   **5 MINUTES**   **SERVES 3–4**   **2 HOURS**

250ml (1 cup) rice vinegar
65g (⅓ cup) granulated sugar
1½ tsp salt
¼ white cabbage, shredded
¼ red cabbage, shredded
2 carrots, cut into thin matchsticks
½ cucumber, de-seeded and cut into batons

Put the rice vinegar, sugar and salt into a saucepan over a medium-low heat to gently dissolve the sugar and salt. Once dissolved, remove from the heat.

Put the vegetables into a large glass container and pour over the vinegar liquid, ensuring that all the vegetables are submerged. Cover and place in the fridge, removing after 1 hour to give the vegetables a good mix. Re-cover and return to the fridge. The vegetables will be ready to eat after 2 hours but they will be better if left overnight. Eat within 1 week.

SWEET CHILLI SAUCE

This hugely popular dipping sauce originates from Thailand. Traditionally the chilli sauce was sweetened with fruit or honey. It's now used as a dip for Western Chinese dishes.

2 MINUTES   **8 MINUTES**   **MAKES 1 SMALL JAR**

6 long Thai red chillies
3 red bird's-eye chillies
5 garlic cloves, peeled
200ml (¾ cup) water
1 Tbsp rice vinegar
150g (¾ cup) granulated sugar
1 tsp salt
1 tsp cornflour (cornstarch) mixed
    with 1 Tbsp water

Put the chillies and garlic into a food processor and pulse until finely chopped. Set to one side.

Add the water, rice vinegar, sugar and salt into a saucepan and place over a medium–high heat, stirring gently until the sugar and salt have dissolved. Once dissolved, add the chopped chillies and garlic and simmer for a further 5 minutes. Slowly stir in the cornflour mixture to thicken. Remove from the heat and allow to cool.

Transfer to a sterilised glass jar and refrigerate for up to 3 weeks.

HOISIN SAUCE

A rich, thick and fragrant sauce that sings 'Cantonese' to your taste buds. It's used in many dishes either as a glaze, in marinades or to flavour a sauce in a stir-fry. It's also a fantastic dipping sauce with its hints of Chinese five spice and aromatic garlic.

5 MINUTES   **5 MINUTES**   **MAKES 1 SMALL JAR**

125g (⅔ cup) demerara sugar
250ml (1 cup) water
⅛ tsp cream of tartar
½ tsp lemon juice
3 Tbsp light soy sauce
1 Tbsp dark soy sauce
3 Tbsp smooth peanut butter
3 Tbsp rice vinegar
1 tsp garlic powder
½ tsp Chinese five spice
¼ tsp white pepper
¼ tsp sesame oil

Mix the sugar, water, cream of tartar, lemon juice, light and dark soy sauces, peanut butter, rice vinegar, garlic powder, Chinese five spice and pepper together in a saucepan and place over a low heat. Once all of the ingredients have dissolved, slowly bring to the boil and simmer until the sauce has reduced by a third. Remove from the heat and add the sesame oil.

Allow to cool, then store your hoisin sauce in an airtight jar for up to a month in the fridge.

MUSHROOM STIR-FRY SAUCE

The Chinese have been using mushroom sauce in their cooking for centuries; its savoury flavour is ideal for stir fries and in noodle dishes, and is widely used in Western Chinese dishes across the world.

20 MINUTES   **20 MINUTES**   **MAKES 1 SMALL JAR**

4 medium dried shiitake or Chinese
   mushrooms
250ml (1 cup) boiling water
½ Tbsp oil (vegetable, groundnut
   or coconut)
1 nori seaweed sheet, ground into
   a powder
2 Tbsp light soy sauce
½ Tbsp dark soy sauce
1 Tbsp sugar
¼ tsp salt
1 tsp cornflour (cornstarch)

Rinse the mushrooms under warm water and put into a large bowl. Pour over the boiling water and leave to soak for 15 minutes until soft. Gently squeeze the excess water out of the mushrooms, reserving the liquid for later. Remove and discard the stalks from the mushrooms, then cut the caps into 4 slices.

Heat a wok or non-stick frying pan over a medium heat, add the oil and fry the mushroom slices for 3 minutes. Remove and place to one side.

Place the mushroom liquid, powdered nori, fried mushrooms, soy sauces, sugar, salt and cornflour into a blender and blitz until smooth. Pour the mixture into a small saucepan and gently simmer until the sauce has thickened and reduced by about a third. Remove from the heat and allow to cool.

Store in an airtight container. The sauce can be kept in the fridge for 1 week or in the freezer for up to 3 months.

Storing Tip
Freeze the sauce in ice-cube trays – once frozen, transfer to a ziplock bag kept in the freezer. Defrost only as much as you need each time.

INDEX

A

Asian slaw 134
asparagus with ginger soy 139
aubergines (eggplant):
 stir-fried aubergine with
  sesame seeds 87
 teriyaki bowl 79

B

bamboo shoots:
 dan dan noodles 123
 eight treasure fried rice 100
 Hong Kong crispy noodles
  with mixed vegetables 110
 hot & sour Chinese vegetables
  with mung bean noodles 126
 kung po cauliflower 66
 mini spring rolls 41
 seaweed & tofu soup 23
 stir-fried ho fun 129
 vegetable chow mein 112
 vegetable udon in yellow bean
  sauce with cashew nuts 116
bamboo steamers 12
bao: mock char siu bao with
 pickled Chinese vegetables
 90
 sweet lotus bao 42
beansprouts: beansprouts with
 garlic & onion 141
 mini spring rolls 41
 Singapore rice noodles 122
 udon noodle curry soup 119
 udon noodles with five spice
  tofu 117
beer: Chinese beer-battered
 pakoda 59
black beans: fried tofu with chilli
 & black beans 92
 tofu, pickled cabbage & black
  beans on rice noodles 125
black pepper tempeh with green
 peppers & onions 94
bok choy: bok choy with
  mushroom stir-fry sauce 88
 spiced bok choy 142

stir-fried ho fun 129
bread: Chinese breadsticks 136–7
 phoenix rolls 34
broccoli: Chinese broccoli in
 garlic & ginger sauce 140
 honey rice wine broccoli
  stems 145
 mushroom teriyaki with soba
  noodles 130
 purple sprouting broccoli &
  peanut satay sauce 84
 teriyaki bowl 79
buns: mock char siu bao with
 pickled Chinese vegetables
 90
 sweet lotus bao 42

C

cabbage: Asian slaw 134
 Chinese pickled vegetables 152
 Napa cabbage & tofu soup 27
 Napa cabbage with
  mushroom sauce 144
 potstickers 33
 tofu, pickled cabbage & black
  beans on rice noodles 125
 udon noodles with five spice
  tofu 117
carrots: Chinese orange tofu
  with peppers & pineapple 69
 Chinese pickled vegetables 152
 fried tofu with chilli & black
  beans 92
 Ho Chi Min fried spring rolls 39
 mini spring rolls 41
 mushroom lo mein 115
 potstickers 33
 roll your own summer rolls 36
 seaweed & tofu soup 23
 spice & sour soup 20
 tofu & vegetable samsa 40
 udon noodle curry soup 119
 vegetable chow mein 112
cashew nuts: asparagus with
  ginger soy 139
 cauliflower yuk sung 55

spicy hoisin mixed vegetables
 62
 vegetable udon in yellow
  bean sauce with cashew
  nuts 116
cauliflower: cauliflower fritters 56
 cauliflower steak with a rich
  Chinese gravy 75
 cauliflower yuk sung 55
 crispy chilli cauliflower 95
 katsu cauliflower with
  tonkatsu sauce 76
 kung po cauliflower 66
 Sichuan crisp cauliflower 93
chillies: Asian slaw 134
 chilli salt tofu 72
 chilli stir-fried lettuce 143
 chilli tofu ramen 120
 crispy chilli cauliflower 95
 fried tofu with chilli & black
  beans 92
 kung po cauliflower 66
 Sichuan pepper mushrooms 70
 Singapore rice noodles 122
 spiced bok choy 142
 stir-fried aubergine with
  sesame seeds 87
 sweet chilli sauce 154
 sweet chilli vinegar dip 39
 Sichuan crisp cauliflower 93
 tom yum soup 24
Chinese baked rice 107
Chinese beer-battered pakoda
 59
Chinese breadsticks 136–7
Chinese broccoli in garlic &
 ginger sauce 140
Chinese five spice 9
Chinese leaf see Napa cabbage
Chinese mushroom curry 71
Chinese New Year 17
Chinese orange tofu with
 peppers & pineapple 69
Chinese pickled vegetables 152
chopsticks 12
chow mein, vegetable 112

coconut milk: coconut rice 99
   tom yum soup 24
congee, rice porridge 104
corn cobs: creamed corn soup 26
   Hong Kong crispy noodles
      with mixed vegetables 110
   mushroom lo mein 115
   spicy hoisin mixed vegetables
      62
   stir-fried ho fun 129
   teriyaki bowl 79
   vegetable chow mein 112
   vegetable udon in yellow
      bean sauce with cashew
      nuts 116
courgettes (zucchini):
   cauliflower fritters 56
   teriyaki bowl 79
creamed corn soup 26
crisps, lotus root 52
cucumber: Chinese pickled
   vegetables 152
   soy pickled cucumber 148
curry: Chinese mushroom curry
   71
   Singapore rice noodles 122
   udon noodle curry soup 119

D
daikon radish (mooli): Napa
   cabbage & tofu soup 27
dan dan noodles 123
dipping sauce 44
   OK dipping sauce 46
   sweet & sour dipping sauce 34
   sweet chilli vinegar dip 39
Dragon Boat Festival 17
dumplings: potstickers 33

E
eggplant see aubergines
eggs: phoenix rolls 34
eight treasure fried rice 100
equipment 12

F
festivals 17
fritters: cauliflower fritters 56
   Chinese beer-battered
      pakoda 59
   sesame seed tempura fried
      tofu 47

   tempura veg with dipping
      sauce 44

G
garlic 11
   beansprouts with garlic &
      onion 141
   chilli stir-fried lettuce 143
   Chinese broccoli in garlic &
      ginger sauce 140
ginger 11
   asparagus with ginger soy 139
   Chinese broccoli in garlic &
      ginger sauce 140
   sweet pickled ginger 151
glass (mung bean) noodles:
   Ho Chi Min fried spring rolls 39
   mini spring rolls 41
   roll your own summer rolls 36

H
Ho Chi Min fried spring rolls 39
ho fun, stir-fried 129
hoisin sauce 154
   hoisin glazed tempeh 80
Holy Trinity 11
honey rice wine broccoli stems
   145
Hong Kong crispy noodles with
   mixed vegetables 110
Hong Kong-style noodle soup
   with tofu & Chinese
      vegetables 113
hot & sour Chinese vegetables
   with mung bean noodles 126
hot & sour sauce 126

I
ingredients 9–11

J
jasmine rice 98

K
katsu cauliflower with tonkatsu
   sauce 76
knives 12
kombu seaweed: dipping sauce
   44
kung po cauliflower 66

L
Lantern Festival 17
lettuce: cauliflower yuk sung 55
   chilli stir-fried lettuce 143
   Ho Chi Min fried spring rolls 39
   roll your own summer rolls 36
limes: Asian slaw 134
lotus root crisps 52
lotus seed paste: sweet lotus
   bao 42
   taro, sesame & lotus puk
      puks 50

M
mangetout (snow peas):
   asparagus with ginger soy 139
   Hong Kong crispy noodles
      with mixed vegetables 110
mapo tofu 83
menu ideas 15–16
Mid Autumn Festival 17
mini spring rolls 41
mock char siu bao with pickled
   Chinese vegetables 90
mooli see daikon radish
mung bean noodles see glass
   noodles
mushrooms: bok choy with
   mushroom stir-fry sauce 88
   Chinese baked rice 107
   Chinese mushroom curry 71
   eight treasure fried rice 100
   Hong Kong crispy noodles
      with mixed vegetables 110
   mapo tofu 83
   marinated mushrooms 103
   mushroom lo mein 115
   mushroom stir-fry sauce 9,
   155
   mushroom teriyaki with soba
      noodles 130
   Napa cabbage with
      mushroom sauce 144
   panko mushrooms with OK
      dipping sauce 46
   phoenix rolls 34
   potstickers 33
   rice porridge congee 104
   Sichuan pepper mushrooms 70
   spicy hoisin mixed vegetables
      62
   stir-fried ho fun 129

tom yum soup 24
vegetable udon in yellow
bean sauce with cashew
nuts 116

N
Napa cabbage (Chinese leaf):
Napa cabbage & tofu soup 27
Napa cabbage with
mushroom sauce 144
udon noodles with five spice
tofu 117
potstickers 33
noodles: chilli tofu ramen 120
dan dan noodles 123
Ho Chi Min fried spring rolls 39
Hong Kong crispy noodles
with mixed vegetables 110
Hong Kong-style noodle
soup with tofu & Chinese
vegetables 113
hot & sour Chinese vegetables
with mung bean noodles 126
mini spring rolls 41
mushroom lo mein 115
mushroom teriyaki with soba
noodles 130
roll your own summer rolls 36
Singapore rice noodles 122
stir-fried ho fun 129
tofu, pickled cabbage & black
beans on rice noodles 125
udon noodle curry soup 119
udon noodles with five spice
tofu 117
vegetable chow mein 112
vegetable udon in yellow
bean sauce with cashew
nuts 116
nori seaweed: seaweed & tofu
soup 23

O
OK dipping sauce 46
onions: beansprouts with garlic
& onion 141
black pepper tempeh with
green peppers & onions 94
Chinese mushroom curry 71
orange juice: Chinese orange
tofu with peppers &
pineapple 69

sweet & sour dipping sauce 34
oven steamed rice 98

P
pakoda, Chinese beer-battered
59
pancakes: griddled sweet
potato pancakes 49
spring onion pancakes 30
panko breadcrumbs: katsu
cauliflower with tonkatsu
sauce 76
panko mushrooms with OK
dipping sauce 46
peanut butter: hoisin sauce 154
peanut sauce 36
purple sprouting broccoli &
peanut satay sauce 84
peas: creamed corn soup 26
peppers: black pepper tempeh
with green peppers & onions
94
chilli salt tofu 72
Chinese beer-battered
pakoda 59
Chinese orange tofu with
peppers & pineapple 69
eight treasure fried rice 100
fried tofu with chilli & black
beans 92
Ho Chi Min fried spring rolls 39
hot & sour Chinese vegetables
with mung bean noodles 126
kung po cauliflower 66
roll your own summer rolls 36
Singapore rice noodles 122
teriyaki bowl 79
vegetable chow mein 112
phoenix rolls with sweet & sour
dipping sauce 34
pickles: Chinese pickled
vegetables 152
sweet pickled ginger 151
pineapple: Chinese orange tofu
with peppers & pineapple 69
potstickers 33
puk puks, taro, sesame & lotus
50
purple sprouting broccoli &
peanut satay sauce 84

R
radishes see daikon radish
(mooli)
red cabbage: Asian slaw 134
Chinese pickled vegetables 152
rice: Chinese baked rice 107
coconut rice 99
eight treasure fried rice 100
jasmine rice 98
oven steamed rice 98
rice porridge congee 104
seasoned glutinous rice 106
sticky rice parcels 103
rice vinegar 9
Chinese pickled vegetables 152
sweet chilli vinegar dip 39
sweet pickled ginger 151
rice wine 9
honey rice wine broccoli
stems 145
roll your own summer rolls 36

S
samsa, tofu & vegetable 40
sauces: dipping sauce 44
hoisin sauce 154
hot & sour sauce 126
kung po sauce 66
mushroom stir-fry sauce 155
OK dipping sauce 46
peanut satay sauce 84
peanut sauce 36
rich Chinese gravy 75
sweet & sour dipping sauce 34
sweet chilli sauce 154
scallions see spring onions
seaweed see kombu seaweed;
nori seaweed
sesame oil 9
sesame seeds: Asian slaw 134
chilli tofu ramen 120
sesame seed tempura fried
tofu 47
stir-fried aubergine with
sesame seeds 87
taro, sesame & lotus puk puks
50
Sichuan pepper 9
Sichuan pepper mushrooms 70
Singapore rice noodles 122
slaw, Asian 134
soups 16–27

creamed corn soup 26
Hong Kong-style noodle
   soup with tofu & Chinese
   vegetables 113
Napa cabbage & tofu soup 27
seaweed & tofu soup 23
spice & sour soup 20
tom yum soup 24
udon noodle curry soup 119
veggie wonton soup 21
soy sauce 9
   hoisin sauce 154
   mushroom stir-fry sauce 155
   OK dipping sauce 46
   soy pickled cucumber 148
spice & sour soup 20
spiced bok choy 142
spicy hoisin mixed vegetables 62
spinach: veggie wonton soup 21
spring onions (scallions) 11
   beansprouts with garlic &
      onion 141
   Chinese beer-battered
      pakoda 59
   crispy tofu with spring onions
      65
   mini spring rolls 41
   potstickers 33
   spring onion pancakes 30
spring rolls: Ho Chi Min fried
      spring rolls 39
   mini spring rolls 41
   tofu & vegetable samsa 40
steamers 12
sticky rice parcels 103
stir-fried ho fun 129
strainers/sieves 12
summer rolls 36
sweet & sour dipping sauce 34
sweet chilli sauce 154
sweet chilli vinegar dip 39
sweet lotus bao 42
sweet pickled ginger 151
sweet potatoes: Chinese beer-
      battered pakoda 59
   griddled sweet potato
      pancakes 49
   tofu & vegetable samsa 40
Sichuan crisp cauliflower 93

T
taro, sesame & lotus puk puks 50
tempeh: black pepper tempeh
   with green peppers & onions
   94
   hoisin glazed tempeh 80
   mock char siu bao with
      pickled Chinese vegetables
      90
tempura: sesame seed tempura
   fried tofu 47
   tempura veg with dipping
      sauce 44
teriyaki: mushroom teriyaki with
   soba noodles 130
   teriyaki bowl 79
tofu: chilli salt tofu 72
   chilli tofu ramen 120
   Chinese orange tofu with
      peppers & pineapple 69
   crispy tofu with spring onions
      65
   fried tofu with chilli & black
      beans 92
   Ho Chi Min fried spring rolls 39
   Hong Kong-style noodle
      soup with tofu & Chinese
      vegetables 113
   hot & sour Chinese vegetables
      with mung bean noodles 126
   mapo tofu 83
   Napa cabbage & tofu soup 27
   phoenix rolls 34
   seaweed & tofu soup 23
   sesame seed tempura fried
      tofu 47
   spice & sour soup 20
   tofu & vegetable samsa 40
   tofu, pickled cabbage & black
      beans on rice noodles 125
   tom yum soup 24
   udon noodles with five spice
      tofu 117
   veggie wonton soup 21
tom yum soup 24
tomatoes: Chinese baked rice 107
   sweet & sour dipping sauce 34
   tom yum soup 24

U
udon noodles: dan dan noodles
   123
   udon noodle curry soup 119
   udon noodles with five spice
      tofu 117
   vegetable udon in yellow
      bean sauce with cashew
      nuts 116

V
vegetable chow mein 112
vegetable udon in yellow bean
   sauce with cashew nuts 116
veggie wonton soup 21
vinegar: soy pickled cucumber
   148
   sweet chilli vinegar dip 39

W
water chestnuts: cauliflower yuk
   sung 55
   dan dan noodles 123
   hot & sour Chinese vegetables
      with mung bean noodles 126
   kung po cauliflower 66
   mini spring rolls 41
   mushroom lo mein 115
woks 12
wonton wrappers:
   veggie wonton soup 21

Y
yellow bean sauce, vegetable
   udon in 116
yuk sung, cauliflower 55

Z
zucchini *see* courgettes

ACKNOWLEDGEMENTS

I have a sneaking suspicion that my mum and my dad knew exactly what they were doing when they opened a restaurant and takeaway with living accommodation above for us (the Wan children). Watching my parents work so hard all the way through my childhood and adult life taught me that anything was possible, but that you had to persevere and put the effort in to achieve your goals. The biggest lesson I learned was resilience; I've seen my parents at the very top and at the very bottom and then back at the top, time and time again. Not once did they ever give up, I just don't think it's in the Wan DNA. I cannot thank them enough for moulding me to be the person I am today.

This book would not have happened without the support and belief of Sarah Lavelle and my publishing agent Clare Hulton; thank you so much for giving me the opportunity to share my life through the food that I cook.

And lastly, to all you foodie fans out there, thank you so much for not only buying my books but also for engaging in all of the projects I'm involved with. Having people out there who I haven't even met but who still truly believe in me is something very special.

K'Wok 'n' Roll
Kwoklyn

www.kwoklynwan.com

Kwoklyn Wan is a chef and broadcaster. He learnt the tools of his trade working in his family's Cantonese restaurant in Leicester. Kwoklyn now teaches and demos Chinese cooking, and is a martial arts instructor.